ANGELS OF FIRE
An Anthology of Radical Poetry in

C000292659

ANGELS OF FIRE

An Anthology of
Radical Poetry in the '80s

EDITED BY SYLVIA PASKIN,
JAY RAMSAY & JEREMY SILVER

Chatto & Windus LONDON

Published in 1986 by
Chatto & Windus Ltd, 40 William IV Street
London WC2N 4DF

All rights reserved. No part of this publication
may be reproduced, stored in a retrieval system, or
transmitted in any form, or by any means, electronic,
mechanical, photocopying, recording or otherwise,
without the prior permission of the publisher.

British Library Cataloguing in Publication Data
Angels of fire: an anthology of radical poetry
  in the 80s.
  I. Paskin, Sylvia   II. Ramsay, Jay
  III. Silver, Jeremy
  821'.914'08   PR6066.A76/

ISBN 0-7011-3074-1

Selection and Introduction Copyright © Angels of Fire 1986

Phototypeset by Wyvern Typesetting Limited, Bristol
Printed in England by
Redwood Burn, Trowbridge, Wilts

CONTENTS

VI The Syntax of Vision

The editors would like to thank the following past and present members of the 'Angels of Fire' collective for their help in making this anthology possible: Gillian Allnutt, Taggart Deike, Ken Edwards, Geoffrey Godbert, Lindsay MacRae, Cheryl Moskowitz, Michèle Roberts, Penelope Toff, Mandy Williams, and the following for their help in arranging various 'Angels of Fire' events: Alasdair Cameron; Julie Parker, Mavis and all the others at the Drill Hall Arts Centre; Jeremy Gibson and the BBC 'Open Space' team; The Arts and Recreation Committee of the GLC; Alan Tomkins; Charlie Rossi; Laurence Baylis; Olwen Ellis at Greater London Arts; The London Borough of Camden; Pamela Clunies-Ross at the National Poetry Centre; *City Limits* magazine; Jonathan Vickers and Toby Oakes at the National Sound Archive; and Lewis Nicholson for his excellent design work.

INTRODUCTION

This anthology brings together a wide variety of forceful and committed energies at work in poetry now. From the outset in 1982, the 'Angels of Fire' collective has provided a meeting ground for a large number of radical poets. It has created an influential sense of community within a wide range of emotions and personal circumstances. Of course such a book is bound to be selective, and as editors we make no claims to be definitive; this is not *the* book of radical poetry. But it introduces a rich and neglected flood of writing that flows from sources far broader than the writing conventionally understood as 'British Poetry'. It surfaces in political struggles and communities in struggle, the women's movement, movements for Black Liberation, anti-nuclear protests; struggles where passions run deep and where goals are visible but elusive to the grasp. Voicing the feelings and desires of many has an important consolidating role – it is not simply preaching to the converted.

This is poetry of affirmation and of resistance. Paradoxically, poetry still lingers in many people's minds as something academic and inessential. In presenting this anthology we hope at least to demonstrate that poetry is neither dusty nor dull, nor easily dismissed. Radical poetry in this country over the last twenty-five years has undergone a determined renaissance which has continued with renewed vigour into this decade. This anthology shows poetry that is alive in people's voices as it shouts, protests, meditates, suggests, and looks to the future.

'Angels of Fire' grew out of the work of several individuals who came together almost by chance to form the first Angels collective. In 1982, Mandy Williams started London's first and only regular poetry cabaret, 'Apples & Snakes', which has always emphasised the work of humorous and political performers. Michèle Roberts was simultaneously developing the coverage of poetry at *City Limits* magazine where she worked to great effect as poetry editor. Penelope Toff and Jeremy Silver were, on a shoestring budget and a Gestetner duplicator, producing the first issues of the magazine *Strange Mathematics*, which features writings and views coming from the alternative side of poetry and fiction. Sylvia Paskin and Jay Ramsay were staging one-off poetry events called 'Knife In the Light', which formed small-scale prototypes for what the 'Angels of Fire' festivals would become. *Knife in the Light* was also the title of a stage-poem written by Jay Ramsay and directed by Taggart Deike which was staged at the Cockpit Theatre, and provided the first half of each evening's programme during the first festival in February 1983.

'Angels of Fire' got going very quickly. We persuaded *City Limits* magazine to sponsor the first festival and this support – which was also extended to the second festival later the same year – gave the events some much needed publicity. Essential, if minimal, funding was gratefully received from the GLC and Greater London Arts. Funding is a constant difficulty we have encountered, 'too little – too late' being the usual story.

Yet from the outset, 'Angels of Fire' presented an extremely diverse programme of poets in performance, who represented nearly every aspect of the new and mainly young poetic energies at work around the country. We summed up the nature of our work in the phrase 'the poetry of engagement' and it was in this spirit that we presented such performers as Joolz, James Berry, H. O. Nazareth, Alison Fell, Valerie Bloom and Paul A. Green. It has been a main commitment of the collective from that time onwards to present in equal proportion the poetry of women and men, and poets from ethnic minorities and communities of shared interest.

We also tried to support as many lesser known poets as we could. From the beginning, it was our policy to have open sessions each night, to which anyone could turn up, participate and have an audience. This element of involvement has given each of the three festivals staged so far a tremendous sense of in-gathering. All of us had the feeling that, albeit for only a short time, a real community of poets could exist and gain from each other's interest in writing and performance: supporting one another and learning from one another.

In 'Angels of Fire 2' (subtitled 'poetry pure and applied') which took place in November 1983, we wanted to extend the scope of our initial work. The collective had expanded with the arrival of Gillian Allnutt, who had replaced Michèle Roberts as poetry editor at *City Limits*; Geoffrey Godbert who had previously been producing a magazine and a press called 'Only Poetry'; and Ken Edwards editor of the innovative and experimental poetry journal *Reality Studios*. (Mandy Williams left us at that time to devote more energy to the increasing demands of 'Apples & Snakes'.) The new collective decided to go broader and deeper in the second festival. Deeper in the sense of trying to suggest a longer time-scale for the existence of radical poetry (we invited established 'outsiders' like David Gascoyne and Roy Fisher), and broader so as to explore the ways in which the whole notion of poetry is extended by interacting with other media. So we included dancers and performance-artists like Hazel Carey, Patricia Bardi and Chris Cheek, video artists like Jez Welsh and Tamara Krikorian, and musicians like Lol Coxhill. We also held nightly workshops on, for example, poetry and the anti-nuclear movement led by the performance group 'Sister Seven', or on 'inner-sound' led by the spiritual linguist Peter Wilberg. The festival extended over two weeks continuously and was probably the largest of its kind to have taken place in this country.

'Angels of Fire 3' was organised by yet another version of the collective. With the departure of Gillian Allnutt, Geoffrey Godbert, Penelope Toff and Ken Edwards, and the arrival of Cheryl Moskowitz and Lindsay MacRae, 'Angels of Fire' was able to retain its high standards of variety, performance and organisation. The third festival was held at the Drill Hall Arts Centre for a week in March '85. The first two nights were filmed by the BBC for an Open Space programme over which we had some editorial control. Two programmes in fact emerged from the festival, both of which were mainly put together by Sylvia Paskin. The first gives a general introduction to our work, the second is set aside for discussion and performance of women's poetry, by women and for women. 'Angels of Fire 3' continued the excitement and activity of the earlier festivals, and in conjunction with the TV programmes and numerous one-off appearances at other festivals and events around the country, we have continued to present the work of many different poets beyond the pull of London's magnet.

All the poets whose work is presented in this anthology have appeared in one or more of the festivals. Our work has always sought to produce 'the meeting and fusion of diverse tongues', as described in our first press-release, and our intention is that this anthology will communicate in the same way – to give pleasure but also to stimulate and to provoke.

All the writers in the anthology are in the process of working towards a definition of radical poetry. In some cases, particularly for black women writers, it is a striking radical departure that their poetry is made visible at all (only last year, Britain saw the first and so far the only anthology of poetry solely by black women writers). For all the writers here, engagement with critical issues and problems is the activity which makes their work new and important. Whilst the term 'radical' has perhaps become over-used in recent years, it is still the only way to describe accurately the work of so many writers on the Left whose poems are represented here. In the forms they adopt, in the sources they use, in their subject-matter and in the demands which are made in their poetry, 'radical' poets are linked both to one another and to a powerful web of movements for change expressing themselves in many different ways. Radical poetry does not necessarily always manifest itself in all of these ways all of the time. But in a steady, considered moving forward new ground is being uncovered, old terrain is being recovered, and a new audience (for whom 'contemporary British poetry' previously held little or no meaning) is suddenly alive to writing that has the power to communicate and even to move people to action in their own lives. The etymology of the word 'radical' indicates a return to essentials and to the roots as part of the idea of change, and this is an important aspect of what is taking place in contemporary radical writing.

There are many different poetries which each contribute to the collective existence of the radical, but a primary shared quality is the consciousness of poetry as political action. Whether it be in the work of a poet like Gandhi vs The Daleks, whose work engages directly and exuberantly on almost a fantasy level with day-to-day life in inner cities, or whether it is in the work of a more introspective poet such as Janet Sutherland, the reader or audience is made aware that political realities concern these writers – not cold concepts of art distanced or abstracted out of all relevance to our present existences. For radical poets, the poem is not simply an object to be admired and crafted, it is also part of a process of change. There is always an awareness that every poem has a political meaning (however personally it may seem to be expressed) both for the writer and the reader. The dynamic at work between these two is as much a political relationship as an aesthetic and a spiritual one.

In one poem, Jackie Kay writes:

England still gives prizes
to princesses who preach
the New Missionary Tongue
in the tone of a Memsahib
the old slaveholder philosophy
and she wants to call this Aid?

(from 'Prizes')

The sense of outrage and rejection is strong here; England as a colonial influence has clearly not changed. But even by making the statement with strength and purpose, Jackie Kay makes a different way of living become a possibility. The potential for change begins to occur in the poem. Frederick Williams makes a related demand in another poem:

> Giv us more space
> Meck wi show wi face pon telly
> Meck we hear wi voice via wireless

> (from 'More space')

Frederick Williams' work, along with many other black writers, reasserts the richness of black culture and the political space which is its right and which it has been so repeatedly denied. In the expression of the demand, the space begins to be made possible, it begins to be created. No-one has any illusions about the huge leap necessary between publication or performance of a poem and the solution to problems in – for example – the inner city or the third world. The need to develop a positive and valid space in which black culture (and indeed every minority culture) can express itself is a fundamental step yet to be taken. For many of the poets here it is a primary requirement before any wider political or spiritual changes can be brought about.

The familiar notion of political art as agit-prop in which obvious targets are the main subjects of the work is extended in radical poetry into an area which allows for beauty, agitation and eventually transformation – such as is seen in John Agard's poem 'Resources'. Poetry and politics are no longer mutually exclusive, and in the new directions of radical poetry the two rarely become crude or dull merely because they are worked together.

There is little room for complacency in the writing presented here, even as it is involved in confronting and questioning the political status quo, so the writing frequently questions its own status as engaged art and as action. In Janet Dubé's poem 'when it's a fine day' (which is from her sequence *1982 A Lament*) the incessant questions relate directly to the problem of what kinds of action one person can take against the threats that face their community. Whether it be in speaking out against sexist attitudes, racism or against the nuclear threat, the poetic articulation of anger and fear is an important communicative step towards isolating and finding ways to overcome those forces of oppression which most deeply affect us. It is a striking realisation that when faced by the most impersonal, mechanistic and apparently all-powerful of threats, it is poetry which resurfaces among the arts as a dynamic medium of importance to those involved in protest and opposition. It is perhaps because the whole nature of newly radical opposition has been characterised by non-violence and direct personal actions, for example the protests (led by women at Greenham) against nuclear weapons, that poetry has been returned to as an important and viable force for change.

But this new-found respect for the value of poetry always contains the paradoxical recognition of its very human fragility. Lotte Moos urges us:

> Think, how many spindles of joy
> Can dance on the point of a needle
> Against grim gravity's pull
> – How many, O Lord, how few?
>
> (from 'Joy')

A sense of dancing freedom and sheer joy is articulated here with an accompanying sense of painful precariousness. The poem takes oppression to be as 'natural' as 'gravity's pull' and the sense of dancing 'on the point of a needle' encapsulates the ambiguous feeling generated by being celebratory in adverse circumstances. This is close to the spirit of the final lines of a poem by Janet Sutherland which urges:

> pull the long roots of aggression
> make a good soup from the nettle
>
> (from 'Spent a day in talk')

Half-literal, half-metaphoric, her poem invokes more than an abstract thought. It is physically involved in making transformations, using its own form as a model for broader change. There is an urgency in the voices which are represented here because, as Tony Lopez puts it:

> No one will
> Speak of this unless we speak –
>
> (from 'Hart's-tongue')

It is noticeable that in the poetry of criticism and opposition a satirical, colloquial and more abrasive discourse is often adopted – for example, by Donal Carroll:

sobbing soubrettes sartorial stimulants
the socially biodegradable

(from 'Rum runner')

In poetry which is more affirmative, however, it is lyrical, more intuitive language which predominates, as in this extract from a poem by Michèle Roberts:

frost on the pavement
edge, evening air a chilly second
skin, my mouth
open, the wind in my throat
desire quickening me.

(from 'On Highbury Hill')

Whilst these two different tones also reflect differences in the styles of male and female poetry, there are signs in some of the poems collected here that this emphasis may be beginning to shift.

When bringing together such a diverse collection of poetries as make up the radical domain, there is a strong temptation to lump them all under the heading 'radical poetry' and look no further. But another of the overarching factors which unifies the work presented here is its emphasis on articulating a sense of 'difference'. Whereas in the sixties many people were striving to show how equal they could be in making love and peace together, radical writers in the mid-eighties have responded much more sensitively to the culture, roots and history of particular communities. Oppression itself has become clear in the many ways in which personal identity is effaced by the conventions and stereotypes constantly projected by the mainstream media. The very substance of individual identity has begun to be understood by radical writers in the retracing and recovering of each of our different histories. It is perhaps only in recognising that there is 'no common ground' that we can begin to set about achieving common goals.

In the sixties and early seventies the great surge of literary energy emanating from America, which produced so much excitement in poetry, was based on – among other things – a powerful attempt to unify a vision of the world. Many writers described a new-found Blakean sense of liberation as they sought to create the 'united states of mind' which would somehow resolve all conflict and end all wars. Flying on feverish economic optimism and rose-tinted hippy ideology, the serious and the pop poetry of the period tried to dissolve what it understood to be the barriers or obstacles which separate ordinary peace-loving people from each other. Urban bourgeois values were seen as a main source of alienation, while Vietnam and the fear of global nuclear destruction were the phenomena which could surely render us all equal under one dominating threat.

Writers like Allen Ginsberg and Denise Levertov remain striking voices today – their poetry retains its power, vision and relevance from which writers in the eighties can clearly follow on. The poetry being written now could not have taken the form it does without their example and the example of their contemporaries in the UK and the USA. The poetry in 'Angels of Fire' is only possible because of the visions and illusions of writers in that period, but there is far greater recognition now both of the difficulty of our task, and of the pain and separation which we may have to go through before our desires can be fulfilled.

Roger McGough's poem 'At Lunchtime A Story of Love' is a typical example of an earlier attempt to draw 'everyone' together into a loving unity as a result of terrible fears, with a hope that in making love we could somehow offset the vague and distant evil that beset us. It is a poem which still amuses and delights its audiences. But in the end for all its deliberately naive sense of optimism it trivialises real fears of a nuclear holocaust and effaces the questions of race, gender and class which confirm individual identities yet also subject them to the oppression of others. One of the main objectives of much of the poetry in this anthology is to encourage readers to explore for themselves their own community and the complexities of identity, and to break down the stereotyped banalities of McGough's commuters on a bus.

This is not to suggest that the radical poetry of the eighties is narrowly individualistic. On the contrary, the poetry collected here is generated out of a deep sense of community and a strong desire to uncover the riches and variety of ways of life hitherto condemned as unworthy or incapable of 'valid' forms of cultural and political expression.

Many of the writers presented here work closely with youth groups, workshops, small press publications or in performance venues which are alive and vital precisely because no mainstream voice (poetic or otherwise) really reflects or gives any support to their experience. Small press publishing still provides the most important, and indeed the only, outlet for new and innovative voices. While remaining solidly ignored by conventional retailers, it continues to receive relatively wide informal circulation, but has its validity consistently eroded by being shut out from the majority of bookshops.

The worlds of the poetry performance, the small press publisher and the local community-centre poetry-workshop are closely related to the writing represented here. By the same token, it is distinguished by its exclusion from the pages and venues of Britain's so-called poetry 'establishment'. Poetry has again become a communal act. It is a much-needed means of validating individuals' identities and histories that are at best ignored and at worst actively repressed by those who hold established power in art and politics. But this poetry is not a happy escape-valve for 'hot air' that builds up in the ghetto. It is literary activism that confronts the forms of oppression which are perhaps more covert today than fifteen or twenty years ago but which are still as powerful. Slavery may have been abolished in the USA, but from a historical perspective it only vanished very recently and the attitudes which preserved it for so long are still very much alive in this country as well as in the born-again US of A. It is these threatening attitudes, whether they exist in the public domain or are constructed in the ideology of individual discourse and personal relations, which radical poetry is joining many other forms of expression to combat and to eradicate.

The seventies saw developments in writing and theory which fed and influenced aspects of radical poetry. By the middle of the decade the glow of sixties optimism had almost completely faded, but avant-garde and free-form writers in this country had already confirmed their interest in the poetry of the American 'objectivists' like William Carlos Williams, Charles Olson, George Oppen, and Charles Reznikoff. William Burroughs' cut-ups and Brion Gysin's experiments with automatic writing added to a growing interest in Britain in the exploration of syntax, disjuncture and linguistically self-conscious writing which was of great density. It often seemed almost surreal, it was often very obscure and perhaps in the end it had less kinetic energy than had been seen popularly before.

One important breakthrough was the appointment of Eric Mottram, a leading British experimentalist poet and academic, as editor of the Poetry Society's *Poetry Review* in 1971. The National Poetry Centre became a site of real innovation and poetic activity, small press publications flourished, and for a time it looked as if the sterile English mode of neo-conservative writing had been banished for ever. Performance-art was becoming increasingly involved with poetry, and there was a lot of new work of considerable interest being written especially by poets like Lee Harwood, Jim Burns and Mottram himself. Others such as Chris Torrance, Alan Jackson and Allen Fisher, who are included in this anthology, are still writing out of that energy-source. But in the intervening years they have each in different ways developed more accessible and more widely communicable forms of poetry. They have succeeded – where others have failed – in avoiding the cul-de-sac of obscurantism into which much of the poetry from that time slowly disappeared.

The radical attack on conventional syntax, and the forceful challenge to conventional forms of constructing meaning, were pursued vigorously by the experimental poets of the mid-seventies. Almost inevitably, as the work they were doing began to take hold, so the establishment took fright. In an unprecedented departure from its 'hands-off' policy, the literature department of the Arts Council of Great Britain dissolved the editorial board of *Poetry Review* – an act which for many amounted to blatant cultural censorship. In place of experiment, a bland and ironic kind of poetry was favoured by the Centre and until relatively recently it has continued along this unadventurous course with – as it appears – hands tied by the mediocrity of ACGB literary 'policy'.

The work of Michael Horovitz in organising and presenting live *New Departures* and the 'Poetry Olympics' is another strand in the development of conditions which enabled 'Angels of Fire' to emerge. Since the late fifties Horovitz has been promoting the work of anti-establishment and popular poets. There is little doubt that up until the late seventies, his energy and commitment were crucial to the constant work of counteracting and interrogating the complacencies of the British poetry establishment.

In promoting the work of Stevie Smith, Adrian Mitchell, the Liverpool poets and, later, Linton Kwesi Johnson and James Berry, Horovitz was drawing attention to an anarchic radical tradition which has always been present in this country. The wild, free-flowing improvised fusions with jazz and blues which live *New Departures* and the 'Poetry Olympics' celebrated began as a series of exciting, innovative and daring events. By the early eighties however, it was clear that 'Poetry Olympics' could no longer provide the right kind of environment for a festival of poets performing newly relevant kinds of material. Too many of the same names upon which Horovitz relied reappeared at each event he staged. The sense of innovation was replaced by an awareness that this was becoming an alternative élite, poets playing at pop-stars, whose performances were always unbalanced by their self-promotion as personalities. So while Horovitz's work remains crucial to the development and extension of radical poetry in the UK, and although the events he stages can always provide something interesting and dynamic, many people felt by the early 1980s that a more open and accessible context had to be devised if the presentation of oppositional poetry was not simply to mimic the mainstream in creating its own hierarchies and élites. 'Angels of Fire' has constantly sought to avoid this danger by bringing new, lesser-known poets into our events, whilst maintaining high standards in the poetry.

The late seventies, of course, also produced the anarchic upsurge of punk, and in its various poetic aspects a new force came into being mainly through noise and violence. Punk dramatically changed the nature of poetry both in the writing and in performance. 'Poetry is dead official' declared Seething Wells, one of the first popular ranters of the Bradford group, and for many people it certainly was. The ranters, though, appeared to be doing little to resuscitate it – that was not their intention. But it was at least partly as a result of their combative approach that the more complex radical poetry gained space in which to emerge. The raw energy of the live performance, and the total rejection of genteel poetry-recitals and of popular élites, enlarged the possibility of a new live space which could allow much of the radical poetry represented in this book to grow and to become more visible in an open and non-hierarchical atmosphere.

Performance as a form of presentation, and as a strategy for communication, is central to radical poetry. Poetry written for performance is conventionally regarded by academics and the mainstream élite as badly written showbiz, ephemeral in its nature, superficial in its substance and ultimately not to be taken seriously. Yet it is the case that most mainstream poets have failed miserably and mumblingly to put across their own work in the live context of readings and recitals. No wonder so many people have been put off all forms of poetry, when its presentation by 'established' poets has rarely moved beyond sedate mutterings into tweed – and not just tweed.

Drawing on the energy of punks and ranters like John Cooper-Clarke or Joolz, catching a fire from masterful British West-Indian dub-poets like Linton Kwesi Johnson and Benjamin Zephaniah, radical poets have found many ways of opening out their work in performance. It has changed the way in which people are able to engage with poetry; audiences have been learning to listen to material that goes way beyond mere agit-prop in its complexity and substance.

The ability to engage immediately and openly with an audience has been accompanied by the heightening of emotional involvement, the active participation of the audience, and a newly critical response. Audiences of performance poetry are no longer passive consumers, ogling the prophetic brilliance of the age's genius at a distance, but are brought into close contact with the depth and the psyche of the poetry.

Equally, poets themselves have found that the directness and flexibility of performance has changed the way in which poetry is written. The old myth is good and dead that performance of poetry can only succeed with work in a strictly oral tradition. For poets like Chris Cardale or Deborah Levy who perform frequently, the printed form of the work is no longer primary or definitive. The text becomes a voice-print, and to read it is to reinvoke the voice of the performer and to retrieve his or her performance. The *presence* of the poet, the inflections and nuances of his or her voice, the emphases of music and movement remain in the printed text. Whilst poets and audiences have understood and developed these ideas over many years, a critical vocabulary has never been developed to talk about the experiences of poetry in performance. A conservative, academic preference for the printed book has failed repeatedly to take into account the ability of sound recordings, let alone video, to reconstruct for analysis and for entertainment this kind of live event. Very gradually, there are signs emerging that this may be beginning to change.

This emphasis on the performance aspect of radical poetry may seem strangely out of place in a printed introduction to a printed anthology.

But another of the distinguishing features of all the writers presented here is their individual insistence on the careful presentation of their work in print. Whilst every one of these poets may frequently be seen performing his or her work, each retains a respect for poetry as a dual text, to be read in print and to be performed or read out loud.

Through the added discipline of writing for performance and the page, radical poets have begun to demonstrate their tremendous impact on the whole notion of poetry.

In organising 'Angels of Fire' festivals we have always made sure that at least fifty per cent of the performers should be women in order to celebrate the creative and innovative dynamism of their writing. In creating this anthology we have further endorsed this commitment for many reasons.

For hundreds of years the white male literary tradition has been considered the mainstream of writing. Women writers where they did emerge, against all the odds, were usually held to be aberrations; depressed, mad, suicidal and unnatural. In other words, they were suspected of writing only because they could not have a man or children. The more 'dispossessed' they were of what society held to be the rightful accoutrements of womanhood, the full-time commitment to home and family, the more 'possessed' they were considered to be. They were always constructed as the 'other', the 'dark continent', unknowing and unknown, not to say unknowable, and their writing, however brilliant, was usually criticised by the literary establishment for being about trivial, marginal and unimportant subjects. As poets they were not usually interested in writing an epic poem, the 'sublime peak'. Virginia Woolf saw them all in history as casualties. She wrote: 'Who shall measure the heat and violence of the poet's heart when caught and tangled in a woman's body?' Her book *A Room Of One's Own* recounts with deft precision all the problems women have faced, and still to some extent face today, in their struggle for recognition and position in the culture. Women have been divided from one another, trapped and privatised into the domestic and not the public sphere, divided by history which was never 'herstory'.

Very little sense of how great a contribution women have always made to writing and political ideas has emerged until recently. An echoing and barren silence seemed to prevail while Narcissus fell ever-lastingly and morbidly for his own image and images. The Women's Movement has brought tremendous changes and one of the most important has been in terms of women's contribution to writing. Over the last ten to fifteen years many writing groups have been set up where women come together to break the silence and isolation of their lives. They share a sense of celebration and pleasure in the *process* of creation rather than the worship of the artefact. Though the meetings are small-scale and intimate, they have become very widespread.

This collective enterprise – the dialogue of woman to woman, the sharing, communication and support – enabled the groups and then small presses to publish the work. To date, feminist publishing is one of the boom areas of the eighties. Some publishers concentrate on uncovering and rediscovering the women of the past – writers and poets who have been allowed to disappear from the bookshelves – whilst other publishers concentrate on new work. So the women who live and create now, and those that lived and created in the past, are united. At the end of her book, Virginia Woolf wrote: 'The dead poet who was Shakespeare's sister will put on the body which she has so often laid down. Drawing her life from the lives of the unknown who were her forerunners, as her brother did before her, she will be born . . . when she is born again she shall find it possible to live and write her poetry . . .'. Out of this connecting, this communal effort, the potential of female resource and vision is unleashed and a prophecy fulfilled.

Where has this resource and vision directed its formidable energy? For many women poets now, there is a real need and desire to investigate the past, to recuperate women from myth and legend and folk tale, and to re-position in history women who have challenged and disturbed the status quo. Alison Fell, in her poem about Mary Wollstonecraft, writes:

You're here, old bully at my right
ear, storming radically up
to a broken blue place where
girls will grow
unimaginably into themselves.

Similarly, in her poem 'Red Rosa', Deborah Levy writes:

Rosa

red star
lifts up her skirts
scans her belly   Rosa

bright star
wants to love
tonight.   Tomorrow

they club her
to death.   Imagination
to death.

Both poets give powerful human resonance to these two revolutionaries of the heart. Judith Kazantzis writes with delicate insight of Eurydice:

She cries
into the zigzagged shell:
Orpheus come back – you're
wrong, you're in hell,
Orpheus my love, come back.

                        (from 'Eurydice')

The retelling of the myth from Eurydice's point of view explores the limitations of what language has previously constructed, and opens our eyes to the exclusivity and paucity of meaning which we have all inherited.

The interrogation of received meanings and the creation of new ones is shared by all the women in this anthology, black and white – and not just in connection with the past. There is a strong radical commitment to exploring the problems, concerns and themes common to women now. There is still a pressing challenge to authenticate and define what it is to be a woman at all and what it is to be a woman writing poetry today. The vision of the transcendent, androgynous mind will only be resolved when *anima* and *animus* stand in equal relation to each other.

The white male literary preserve, 'that long monologue which they have called dialogue with us', will cease as 'The Three Marias' of the *New Portuguese Letters* suggested. It will have to, since the only real art or literature of any group comes into being when the members of that group stop feeling the need to explain and justify themselves. They must be free to reclaim and create their own culture for themselves.

This ambition to achieve a female aesthetic in poetry has brought about the proliferation of poems by women which perceive and articulate so much that is seminally human, and many subjects which lie outside the experience of men: matters of death such as rape, psychic and physical; separation and exile; and matters concerning life such as sexuality, desire, birth and mothering. There is an undeniable sense of vulnerability and openness often missing in the poems written by male poets.

This vulnerability about themselves, and the willingness to struggle and fight to reclaim and remember so much that has been lost and despoiled, is linked by women to the fate of the whole planet. That is why there are so many poems about the nuclear threat, and why Greenham Common has come to mean so much to people everywhere. Lindsay MacRae in 'Poem from Greenham' writes:

> I push my camera against
> the fence,
> 'Shoot me –
> Shoot me then'
> The soldier makes a peace sign
> then he turns his fingers round
> and pokes his tongue.

The image of woman as fetishised object of desire, hate and fear (all three often inextricably and frighteningly intertwined as in Lindsay MacRae's poem), must be made to fall away and die. With this aim in mind, women poets are restructuring and redefining language itself, giving back to individual words their original meaning or indeed creating new ones. In both cases they are writing radically. They twist and subvert the inherited imagery and language in order to express experiences which the available symbolism and connotations do not fit or contain. To imagine a language is to imagine a world.

There is power and transparency in poetry. At the end of the nineteenth century, the French poet Arthur Rimbaud recognised this when he wrote:

> There shall be poets! When woman's unmeasured bondage

shall be broken, when she shall live for and through
herself, man – hitherto detestable, having let her go –
she, too will be poet! Woman will discover the unknown!
Will her world be different from ours? She will come upon
things that will be strange and unfathomable; repellent and
delightful, we shall take them, we shall understand them.

Rimbaud's prophecy, the second in this introduction, is fulfilled. As
Mary Michaels puts it in 'Dream and Five Interpretations':

> *I am the fear of it*
> *I am the flame*

This is the flame of revolution. The Greek word for poet means 'one
who makes'. Women are indeed the poets now and of the future.

No Conclusion
The themes, ideas, responses and preoccupations of the poetries in this
anthology powerfully reflect on the confused times in which we live. We
are in process and there is evidence of this in the gaps, contradictions
and conflicts explored, expressed and sometimes unresolved in these
poems. There is still so much that separates us from one another. But to
be separated from hope would be intolerable.

Many of the poems in this anthology testify to the outrage and doubt
that human history – which has been lived so far with so much pain and
magnificence – is threatened now as never before. We live in a time
when the future cannot be trusted and we are separated from the
promise of the future. There is no hope for us if we let the spirit die. But
the essence of this poetry is that the spirit cannot die.

ARTHUR RIMBAUD

Translated from the French by Sylvia Paskin

Drunk one morning

Oh I feel so beautiful. I feel so good.
Terror in this beginning but I can't, I won't stop.
Stretched out on a rack but it's different.
The torture is different and exquisite.
Pain not of torture but creation. It obsesses me.

Bravo, Bravo I say for all that has come out of me and is still
To come –
And for my marvellous body. I can feel it.
I can feel it – for the first time.

And I can hear laughter, the laughter of children
From behind their hands
It begins with them and there it will end.

The poison is going to stay inside us, coursing
Through our veins, long after the the trumpets depart and we are
Left standing there, in the road, (back to what we are – not
Joined together by exuberance)
The poison will remain.

You don't believe me, do you? You think we were all born
To be slaves and monkeys forever.
You are wrong.

Passion. That's what we need to make good the promise of what we
Can be, of what we all carry inside us.

To be human, to be more than human and then to be human again.
Passion.

Elegance, knowledge, violence.
Pah.
Their promise. Do you know what their promise was.
To chop down, to cut up, to bury at night in secret
That terrible tree.

What tree
The tree that spreads its darkness everywhere
The tree of good and evil
And their promise was to exile forever those tyrants I abhor.

Decency, respectability, compromise.

Passion, to create absolute pure love

You know what you do, you start with a little – disgust
And you end with a riot of flowers
(because everyone knows you can't eat eternity in one mouthful)

The laughter of children

The people who never try anything
The people who never risk anything
That fear of faces and things
It's all in my head from last night
Beating out its message on the walls of my mind
Struggling to get out

It begins, my friends in barbarity.
And in the end you have angels, angels of fire and ice

Last night, I got drunk – so drunk it left me free
To think.

Oh, Method. We have always used you. Now we want you.
We have faith in poison. We will give everything we have.
Be aware – it's a strange time.

Between waking and sleeping, and sleeping and waking
And this time when the dream comes, we shall finish it.

It is – the assassins' hour.

I

BURNING ISSUES

JANET SUTHERLAND

The view

'. . . And he overthrew those cities, and all the plain, and all the
inhabitants of the cities, and that which grew upon the ground.
  But his wife looked back from behind him, and she became a
pillar of salt . . .'

Genesis 19 25–26

Unlike Lot's wife she turned back

not stone, cold bleached
nor man's mate – nameless woman
not for curiosity
nor pity

not for

at the flash
the balls of her eyes melted

JAY RAMSAY

Dark of a dream

Christ again and again

Christ Christ Christ

As an ice-skater swish-arabesques to a spinning stop –
The rink in the stadium frozen, hard
And Christ was on the cross there
And his pose was so embarrassing
And people were being sick, trying to leave
But they could not they were riveted
As a few staggered across the sand
Covering their adoring faces in His Blood.

It was expertly made.
One matchstick, and a half-a-one: crosswise.
On it, a bleeding black dot

and a column of ants, marching away

JUDITH KAZANTZIS

Memorial: Vietnam
Voices from a TV documentary

It is not we
    Bam?
  And that felt good.
And I wanted more
  I wanted more
    y'know

I wanted to go
  out and kill some
    Gooks
  I wanted to go out
    and kill some
      Gooks
        y'know

no more than a fly

Hey jet, get'em and
  that felt good and
    hey jet, get'em
  and that felt good
and the napalm just dripping off 'em

You take them

My heart just soared
I turned round and looked
            at them
My heart just soared
a bloody good bunch of killers

May you be winners, more
Importantly
in the Biggest Game of All/Life/
Which we All Play

The daily grind   I enjoy it

It was a pretty country
except for the people

   This shitty piece of ground
    I'm dying
      and I can't fucking believe it

... not we
who are the savages
the lives of my countrymen
   are worth no more than a fly
it is not we
You take them
        and swat them
            dead
and that's that   who are the savages
   that's that

   I'm dying
and I can't fucking believe it

JEREMY SILVER

Cloudbursts

I
And the voice begins
to flow with
a sly inflection
the upturned ending
eye-line
darts to the phrase

2
lips of the city
murmur of their own discord
words set free
from smothered pasts
histories unlooked for

in sleep gaze up
into our vulnerable faces

I speak and immediately
forget what I said

3
In confusion
I identify them
as the Scribes of the Book
they take form before me
I see their flat features
slowly rising
coming up to my face
their warning utterances
sage prophecies –

how do we begin
and end actions
out of this
unreliable language?

4
in the autumn
the cracked frost radio
bristles porcupines
ostensibly a voice
talks Egyptology
counsels safety
in the sharp international
ice-feathered air

5
now that we have a philosophy
with which to reduce reality
we are still less able
to respond to the threat
of its imminent destruction

6
In confusion
in stillness
the tendons and sinews
of the land
stand out in ridges
fears hold our breath
take giant strides
across the country

the voice of the radio
steals away

7
we are all busy we say
we work in the fields
setting up boundary stones
which mark our land

the harvest is full
and must be brought in
shift earth shift
we are marking boundaries

the storm approaches
our eyes rise up
to the darkness
and do not disturb us
we are all busy
making divisions
setting up stones

the buckwheat is high
and must be cropped
the clouds assemble
the sky fills with fear

and we are all busy
our backs are all bent
we keep our ears to the ground

8
as spilled ink
on ancient manuscripts
our progress obscures
the scribes' crucial words

9
How much danger a tyrant risks
before the people refuse?

in proportion to his deceit
the food he steals
the paths he stops
the strength of fear he unleashes?

10
on the wall
inside today
watery sun casts
faint shadows of sparrows
nervously watching
chipping at food
grappling with the air

11
in the attempt fallen
to recapture the dream
sleep overtook them
as does the language
of war

stopping us speaking
to each other
road-blocks
stopping us
reaching each other

12
that way they have
of making me talk back
out loud
in the way that
makes me cry
makes me need to

13
we try to re-create
it all seems pointless
since Monday
I have been paralysed
everyone is frozen
since the missiles came

the date of each event
becomes important
although this record
would be lost
with all the others

each of our perspectives
is forcibly altered
disturbance in the field

very hard to see
what counts now
except to try
to stop the shouting between us
to stop their cold
blooded progress

MICHELENE WANDOR

intimations of violence

commando blindfold
                bound
                        blindmarch bearded

the land a family belongs to
                        becomes belonging
to another family
the families fight
the land smiles
under their feet

the commando knows each stone
each twig each thistle knows
the stump where prickly pears
bloom
        you don't have to be a liberal
to regret the continuing
of hostilities

you don't have to be a revolutionary
to want peace
commandos don't have to be men

remote islands
don't have to shiver

JOHN AGARD

Resources

The night is a dark continent
gleaming with natural wealth
precious bigness of moongold
and ore of starlight

From behind conference room windows
multi-national companies point vested
questions towards the heavens

How can we drill the sky
How can we smelter the stars
How can we convert the moon
to jewellery

They draw up plans to exploit the night
They drink to the future of this dark continent
They wish each other sweet dreams of investment

JANET DUBÉ

(when it's a fine day'

when its a fine day
and the house is quiet
and I'm on my own

when the fire gets low
as the cat kills a bird
and the sun is blazing

on the daffodils,when
the chickens scratch
and cluck,scratch

and cluck,and the house
is quiet and the sun
is blazing on the rockery

when the pale mauve
anemones are open to the sun
and the blue green daffodils

unsheath to yellow
in the blazing sun
when the house is quiet

and the chickens scratch
and cluck and the lambs
learn to eat grass

when the blue green
daffodils unsheath to yellow

as the jets scream overhead

should I plant onions
or write a poem?Shall
I plant flowers or read

the paper?would it
be better if I had a job
or is that part of the war

machine?is it better
to be certain
or uncertain?if I do

something for peace
does it help?if I do
something for peace

does it help peace
or does it help me?
if I do nothing
what does that mean?
tell me,its the one thing
I ever wanted to know,tell
me this one thing and I'll
never ask again,tell me
the truth,its what I want
to know,I need to know,
tell me,how am I joined
to the war machine,tell me

can I get off?

CHERYL MOSKOWITZ

Protecting life

A woman sat
  belly rounded
with a sign hung round her neck
and a collection box at her feet
I AM PROTECTING LIFE, it said

There were some, not many, who gave without question
Money, they said
to feed her coming child –
for it is always the children who will suffer
  There were others who said No
we must feed the woman
or she will not move to use your money
she will starve
But she did not open her mouth for the food
to be put in.

Why will you not eat, they cried
I am protecting life, she said.

And then,
  the others: Here, see, our money – take our money

Life cannot be bought, she said

and still she sat
voluminous, a sphere containing histories and futures
and somewhere inbetween,
the essence.

How can we help, What can we do?
the well-wishers squirmed and wriggled
Perhaps it is clothes she needs, blankets to keep warm

And then someone said no. We must make signs
and show her that we support her

We, too, will wear placards
and they hung them, carefully

over their cravats and next to their pearls
SHE IS PROTECTING LIFE, they said
and watched her
constantly, for signs.
Will she be happy now? Can we move her
Surely this was what she wanted
But still she sat. The world was heavy with her presence
and the people were worried.
They had done what they could and still
they could not move the woman.

I AM PROTECTING LIFE, she said, and did not budge

She is too big, too present, they said
We need her space
for industries
for factories and power plants
for progress
and, when finally they could do no more
the judges came
in robes and wigs, arriving like dark angels
Gentle persuasion is what is needed
Arbitration, sighed the court, and gave the message to the people
The land is not yours, they told her
It is common land, she smiled – I'm protecting life

and all at once
she groaned and moved herself onto all fours
and slowly, warmly
deliciously, she opened out like a flower
and her leaves and petals flooded the streets and towns
and cities
with redness
and life.

KEN EDWARDS

Lexical dub, for Sarah Tisdall

Secret secret never seen
secret secret ever green
                    Popular song

Police glossolalia haunt radio heavy wind
Instruments of use in time of war
From here to Texas burgeoning

An offence an offence (as officially defined)

We wage war on all the animals that come to live with us

An offence such an offence

Teams finger ethics of punishment
A gunboat to Morocco had become an epidemic
On blood red screen man washes car w/ hosepipe
That person shall be guilty of a misdemeanour
Approaches or is in the neighbourhood of or enters
Each occupied square is surrounded by 8 squares

Any prohibited place possession or control

Looks like colour xerox & feels like a total effect

Any sketch plan model article note document
Or information like when real blood appears
On video screen music
Swells to gothic cancerous zombies superimpose
If any person communicates or retains he
Shall be liable to imprisonment with or without
Hard labour Any work of defence arsenal factory
Dockyard camp ship telegraph or signal station or office
Demand right of reply on behalf of the conservative party

Any ship arms or other materials or instruments
Of use in time of war or any plans or documents
Demand paralysis respect for rule of law
Any railway road way or channel

The Agadir crisis, 1911

Declared by a Secretary of State to be a prohibited place
Shall be a prohibited place

*

Edition of   Starts with £5 scag bags on the council estates
'The London   Or any place used for gas water or electricity works
Programme'   Ends with novocaine mainlined into tongues
on heroin
addiction,   To protect official secrets & get us out
transmitted   Of a bad situation *vis-à-vis* that which endures
13.iv.84,   Or any place where any ship arms or other materials
London   Or instruments of use in time of war
Weekend TV

Starts w/ a gunboat to Morocco Ends w/ a blood red
     screen

Starts w/ crystals of bad scag   Ends w/ any prohibited
     place

Starts w/ approaches or is   Ends w/ an offence

Starts w/ ethics of punishment   Ends w/ war

Starts w/ possession or control   Ends w/ war

*

Speech by   Not many months ago we found in the middle of the
Lord   Fortifications at Dover an intelligent stranger
Haldane,   Who explained his presence by saying
1911; see
article by   He was there to hear the singing of the birds
Peter Kellner   Any offence an offence the offence the offence
in *New*   Incites or counsels or attempts to procure
Statesman,
6.iv.84   An offence an offence an offence that offence

Official   2 men got up to speak but both were forcibly pulled
Secrets Act,   down
enacted
22.viii.11,   By their neighbours after they had uttered
after going   Such an offence an offence such an offence
through all
stages in the   A few sentences again they were pulled down
Commons in   By their neighbours the vote 107–10 (500+ abstentions)
less than an
hour

One hot Friday afternoon in August
If a justice of the peace is satisfied
Things went a bit far he may grant a search warrant
Authorising any constable to seize
If necessary by force and to search and to search
Any sketch plan model article note or document
All acts which are offences when committed or when
    committed
Having been or being about to be committed

*

Riots in   In 1981 crucial
Brixton,   Molotov cocktails made white goods blush
Toxteth &   Crunched underfoot in a skin of acid rain
elsewhere,   From here to Texas looks like colour xerox
summer 1981
cf. Sex   No hope   no future
Pistols,   Cancel future with instant response
c.1977   Police cruise total exclusion zone
               Pre-emptive in the service of our (zombie) way of life
Sentence of 6 In 1984 an example must be made
months on   An offence the offence an offence
Sarah Tisdall Include any communicating or receiving
for disclosing Include the copying or causing to be copied
information
on the arrival Between an unquestioned & unquestionable Secret Vote
of Cruise   Include the transfer or transmission
missiles to   Punishable under this Act this Act may be cited
The Guardian In defence of instruments of use in time of war

Document includes part of a document

Numbers of union leaders start to disappear

Model includes design pattern and specimen

Peruvian flutes indicate primitive lisping apparatchiks

Sketch includes any photograph or other mode of
    representing

Dogs give voice in the echoing car-park

Offence under this Act includes
Any act omission or other thing
Which is punishable under this Act

*

See: Duncan Fish stains guttering peach police glossolalia
Campbell, *Big* Identify any person
Brother is Other than a person acting under lawful authority
Listening, Daddy's dead riot squad riot
1981 Notwithstanding that no such act is proved against him
He shall be guilty of felony
Any constable must have a plan for copious stinking
    water
It shall be not be necessary to show that the accused
    person
Was guilty of any particular act
He may be convicted
Before everything disappears everything disappears
Xerox handcoloured by dayglo marker
Political conviction not allowed

A person that person any person
Other than a person acting under lawful authority

In lunar months weeks playing cards alphabet

The offence an offence
An offence an offence
An offence such an offence
An offence an offence an offence that offence
Such an offence an offence such an offence

An offence an offence are offences

If necessary by force

Such an offence

JAMES BERRY

City riot

On and on again through night
of thudding and jawfuls of blood,
of skin of gravel and glass,
quickly bodies change places
in flashes of flames.
And smeared people, gutted
shops, charred billboards,
all make streets
into stoned and trackless woods.

What is this? An outburst
of locked-up skills?
A beating to break
steely forms of establishments
to search for nuggets,
search for the proceeds of trade
of just records of lost days?

Is it a street dance of pain
or substitute movements
for money spending
or merely an impelling
to give way to catastrophe
to blast away pure
human difference as offender?

Involved, yet inactive, you look on.
Smashed lamps darken time.
Networks of violence master
everybody: the rhythms jar
everybody. And everybody is lost:
casual routines suspended.
And around ripped law-men,
undamages faces are twisted.

Is it all to end offensives
of separation? Is it

to summon new days because
humans move as companies of lions
and they are rivers and doves
who cross boundaries without guns?

Is this merely an exercise
for another voice to follow?
Or will the face of mangled streets
in its appeal evoke
nothing more than dead days?

VALERIE SINASON

Round up

Boys and girls come out to play
I call you up now
I am marking the register
of broken nursery rhymes
Are you there?
Are you truanting dear dead ones?

Where is Eddy, Eddy
with his brylcreem ever-ready?

Prince Charming is in the night sky
He revs up on his two-wheeled steed
He revs up at the dead end of the world
His mother has smashed the glass slipper.
Cinderella rocks her cold Borstal feet.

Boys and girls come out to play . . .

Sleeping Beauty burps . . .
under mountains of fat, rivers of gin
Her flesh cries out for silk and jewels,
her flesh cries out for the mouth of a king.

Yvonne is that you?
Yvonne of the bushes,

Yvonne of the grass,
Yvonne of the tits
and the soft white arse?

Oh the Queen of Hearts
was made a tart
they ate her parts away
She took to drink
got thrown in the clink
and rots in Holloway

Boys and girls come out to play
the rain doth piss on Holloway . . .

There is Terry
the frog the princess did not marry
the beast that Beauty did not kiss
He was never allowed to be a prince.

The ugly sisters are thin and white
as cigarettes
They are rising up from their ashtray floors
they are burning out
are worn to a stub.

Oh the children rev up round the sun
the children throw stones at the moon
the children are hurled off the tower blocks
on a saturday afternoon.

Mary, Mary, Mother Mary
how does your garden grow?
With crosses, canes and legal reins
and nursery rhymes breaking in a row, ho, ho,
and nursery rhymes breaking in a row.

Boys and girls come out to play . . .

LINDSAY MACRAE

Poem from Greenham

The smoke chokes thick
and slow.
Grief eyed we wait for tea.

The town is out of bounds
'Lets shoot the lot of them'
Thug ugly – on his soap-stool
propped against the bar
'We know their type
we don't serve them in here'

My mother telephones –
long distance
scared that they'll steal me away
in a night lit by sirens
and helicopter drawl.

Thick as a milkshake
hard as a rifle's butt,
they serenade us from
behind the wire.
They've nothing
that we want.

A man raps on the car
his fist collides with steel
as we skid away.
Should we have stayed
beneath your fat red thumb
to hear the feeble punchline
'Common prostitutes'.

Mud is the victor here
only the mud has won.

I push my camera against
the fence,

'Shoot me –
Shoot me then'
The soldier makes a peace sign
then he turns his fingers round
and pokes his tongue.

We take them on video
They capture us
on celluloid
like Macbeth's vision
'Look at these weird
and unnatural hags'
A picture tells a thousand stories
but it can't explain
how slow time passes
in between the kettle screams.
Like a birthcry
Like a struggle
for the first clear breath.

TAGGART DEIKE

Dear Mum, I missed your funeral today

Dear Mother, I missed your funeral today.
Dark sails have set you on that sea – of unknowingly.
And the clan gathered to see thee off.

We spoke, on the phone, late one night, a few weeks back.
You sent your love to us all. And to me.
It was a word not oft used in the old household.
Love.
Used sparingly.
Nor any of those words of endearment
which I gush all over my children – without thinking . . .
No, that's not true. I ration them, too. Even outwardly.

Martha once sent a letter – years & years ago –
blossoming with thoughts of love, as she was blossoming.

Damon, as well. They of the Sixties . . .
Wanting to heal the world.
Heal. And so they are.
As for the world . . . Well, the earth
– Tim knows of the earth, a plantsman all these years.

Oh dear, we've left you in a rather sad parcel of it, I'm afraid.

I passed there last night, in a fitful sleep.
Only now hearing of your passing – one week late.
I was carried through the canyons,
and thence to that oasis, which even the Mormons abandoned.
Along the expressway where we rode, five years ago, you at the
    wheel.

But last night, I saw nothing else.
Of Man's settlement. Of Stardust, the Dunes, Cesar's Palace
or the sidewalks lined with light bulbs.
The city of light bulbs.

You showed me the warehouses, then. And the homes where people
    live.
The workers. The ship's crew. Polishing buckets of coins.

But last night. Only the road.
The distant hills. A silent place.
The wilderness that a Spaniard, plum loco,
in search of El d'Oro, called . . . Las Vegas.

You could have been buried in Washington, the state,
near Tim & co . . .
near Hanford, the world's first atomic reactor,
and soon, the first US fast breeder reactor.
Good old Wash . . .

You could have been buried in Colorado, Denver – our old
    hometown –
near Martha & co . . .
near Rocky Flats, the world's largest plutonium factory
where gusty winds blow, and seeds & grains of 'plu'
drift down upon the camera crews of 'Dynasty'
– and other local inhabitants.

You could have been buried in San Francisco – 'City By That
  Golden Gate' –
near John & co . . .
near Livermore Laboratories, the armpit of nuclear science,
M-X, Star Wars, W84, bombs and more bombs.

You could have been buried in New York City
near Damon & co . . .
. . . world's number 1 target – the Big Apple, in a Bull's eye.

You could have been buried
near us & co . . .
here in the UK, 'the unsinkable aircraft carrier'
– with NATO's command centre, cementing down in High
  Wycombe;
– with the world's first deployment of Cruise missiles, lumbering
  along the roads;
– with 105 US bases and facilities – at last count;
– with Polaris submarines, bomb factories, 'The Atomic Weapons
  Research Establishment'
—— all well established.

Instead, you've been assigned to a time-space capsule called
  Nevada,
near the atomic weapons underground testing site, USA
(rivalled only by Kazakhstan, USSR).
A fitting description for the poorest-parcel-of-earth of them all:
the *planet* Earth.
Presently the *Galaxy's* leading atomic weapons testing site.

75 years.
Not exactly the best 75 years
to have inhabited the infirmary of old terra firma.

Father Teilhard (Chardin) says that future evolution depends upon
  us
(as opposed to Nature, or divine intervention).

75 years
crisis years
When Man died on the Crux . . . or lived . . . lives.

So little time
to take ... matter ...
into our own hands.

End the ending.
Begin the beginning.

DONAL CARROLL

The worst possible interpretation

1
Gaunt at Gant's Hill,
the prodding presence of his thumb
flicks the cars, windscreen-wiping.

He smokes philosophical tropes,
picking the bones of the weekend
till we reach that campus;
two up   two down
and there's always two to go

2
Skald-sniffing,
the rigours of his voice
have married all the worlds:
food: my stomach ends north of the Bosphorus;
drugs: an adrenalin overdraft;
politics: only an organisation can combat an organisation;
the individual is just dust
without the clothing of the Party;
the isolate strutting towards the centre of the stage.

3
Then the indecent descent
from politics to politesse;
politesse, the stethoscope from the eye
to the ego and blank again.
Intelligence, gleaned from the social,

marooned on the spike
of luscious inwardness;
the final emigration to the inside.

4
Only a strength significantly spent
can be retained
and trained to a demand.

5
Suicide is the choice
of one clubbed choiceless:
the fling of silence when you speak.

II

CEREBRAL DISCO

JAY RAMSAY

Club Monte Solaire

This is a dead concept.

This is a plastic flower.

The hotels are high on emptiness,
Cars hoot impatient and glaring
This air of cool cool ennui.
Palm trees parody Tahiti.
And the heat beats
On lines of parasols & uniform chairs,
By the private or pay-up beaches.

The rich are not different: just distant,
It's a spray-on gloss every capitalist can buy.
And the day that lengthens
With absent tension
And dies, in the end, like any fashion
In a vacuous commercial abstraction –
The way the yachts wait like servants at anchor;
While the girls play detached, à la Paris Match.

This is the South of France;
But there is no spirit here –

The club is a ritual of smooth ejection,
An architectural wonder of psychic vivisection.
Here is your hyper-material future
While the gods observe their bored, cavorting pawns
Like Romans; from the sky.

Boys, beach boys
Golden lads
In minuscule trunks
With bulging pricks on cocktail sticks,
Smirk, smile and stalk
Considering the aesthetics of cunt.

JANET DUBÉ

this is an advertisement

create your own environment
design a space for living
realise your dreams

and to help you   HUMAN WALLPAPER
so new it's almost raw
so real it nearly breathes
and friends will ask 'is it alive?'

although with HUMAN WALLPAPER
who needs friends? no need
to go outside your own front door

a product of the best research
and marketed in different qualities
a grade to suit YOUR way of life –

choose from 'white'
'black' 'coloured' 'other'
'protest' 'primitive' or 'free'

have YOU a social conscience?
for one year only PARTICIPATE
in your own wallpaper

or for the artistic
underdeveloped wallpaper –
finish it off yourself

choose now, pay later!
a percentage of all profits FOR ALL

find yourself, help yourself,
make a name for yourself   in HUMAN WALLPAPER

(embossed with peace
and long-life guaranteed
for happiness FOR ALL)

Psst— heard the one about the middleclass Indian lawyer and a bunch of metal skinned Super Soldiers from the wrong side of outer space?

...NOW READ OFF!!

Well Gandhi turned the other cheek and hoped they wouldn't miss and the Daleks are the kinda critters go for different kindsa kicks / Well up his sleeve had maybe Gandhi also a whole other bunch of tricks and as for the Daleks...

Spot the Lies!!!

SELF DEFENCE
FIRST STRIKE

by Gandhi Versus The Daleks | Just before the end of the Miners' Strike, 85 | (FOR THE NATION'S VISION!)

PLEASE DO NOT ASK FOR MERCY AS A REFUSAL OFTEN OFFENDS

straight to the point: extermination / no need to get inquisitive. these guys dont relate to words like acts of parliament legislative & executive they're what you might describe as the state, the ruling classes, chemical/germ weapons & the bomb all rolled into one.

and having fun

well evidently cos if you look carefully you cant

see a smile spread all over their angelic satanic little countenances and their sweet little head horns wiggle and tremble with delight whenever they dont say "ay ay that's the way dull not device by coldness and delay" & just say "Exterminate!"

They're daleks— not dal-iks/they're not scousers or smart alecs daleks will be daleks/they're not macho or heartless they're really quite harmless/ so long as you're lifeless →

Or dont exist

two possible rules for wordfucking, poetry, cerebral disco, awake-walking or whatever you wanna call it: ① If you dont understand, the first thing to do is suspect the author of incompetence (not yourself immediately, tho you might be stupid).→

These guys are no great orators
— they're things of crushin flesh&blood action
No moans. No fuss. No complaints.   NO TEA BREAKS!
                                     NO STRIKES !
more selfless. than ants — Damn Good At Their Job

hip to laughter & tears & philosophy & compassion & reason
they this for their universe — an Eternal Cosmic Reich
WANT
(you know — small businessmen, nothing complicated)   N O P E !

ordinary guys — plutonium of the earth
they're moderately ambitious   Z E N CAREERISTS YOU COULD SAY WITH RELISH
              + no hang ups you know. no sizzlin secret sorrow
FAMILY MEN + WHAT A FAMILY ——→   THE MEMBERS DO
                                                NOTHING BUT BLAST
NO EGO TRIPPERS or   s&m excrement fetish   THE SHIT OUT OF
                                                ANYTHING AND BARK
             POWER PROBLEMS HERE   'EXTERMINATE'
       IT'S
all for one and one for all/let's enslave'n'kill everyone'n
And they're   Jorkers.Jorkers.Jorkers.Jorkers
              W O R K E R S   !!!?!? have a ball
              it's a workers' state
and daleks are democratic—
   one vote per population CARRIED   and others
                           IMMEDIATELY   wanna have
      and by a b a l l o t   some fun &
that's so secret ITS   they don't like it
           NON-EXISTENT
                        Imperialists?
                        a) It's their backyard
                        b) They gotta spread The
                           Revolution

& andmoreoveralsofurthermoreadditionallyImightadd
they. voz not only obeying orders.   they take
                                     FULL RESPONSIBILITY
this is a Utopian set-up: for their actions — DO I?
                              equality fraternity liberty

Well if you're a dalek you're free to
wipe out entire galaxies for target practise—
can't ask for much more freedom than that, can you?
      well — unless you're somekinda anarchist . ¿EM OD UOY OD !?

no sir these fellows have got class and style
no goosesteppin for peacockin or boomboombeatin on drums
they just see a job to be done — anything living
and try to anihilate it: Exterminate! — Men of their Word!

INSECURITY? INDECISION? VACILLATION? PROCRASTINATION?

These guys have got just 1 journey with 1 destination —
A killer ray comin into your S O U L just to make death to you

The will
Triumphed so long ago, they dont even think to celebrate
Tougher than diamond concrete, they use hard dudes for toeclippers

brush their teeth with iron filings, take showers in giant laceratin liquidizers
and baths in hell hot microwaves
go swim in sulphuric acid before a light breakfast of a few mountains
then it's a workout in the back garden (—we call it the cosmos—)
garglin with domestos
and piranhas for to get the eeee e e   e e eee e JhhhX-ch-ch-EX- EXTERMINATE! sounding right

and straight to the nearest creature (that isn't a dalek) for to
fatally tickle the jugulars

THEY'RE NOT — arrogant
cruel or manipulative

SEX? BOOZERS? Laser scourges in their underpants
Megawatts Into Their Braincells
[note — any allusion to everyday reality (if any) here is, naturally, purely & incidental]

SPACE FOR YOU DEAR READER TO DRAW IN!

racist,
dont persecute gays
+neither are they sexist

And their sense of humour is infectious—
they just kill you everytime

MEGADEATH * is the main man reaper deathweb weaver
& he play for the ultimate finders keepers

Imagine You're the ball (YOU) & he's the keeper
he will not try
to keep you out

and megadeath* is sorta the daleks' triffic catchy collective name & when they mean business, the business is mean that is—perpetually

QUESTIONS!
1) ABORTION ON DEMAND??
2) RESPECT FOR THE FOETUS LIKE A BORN CHILD??
3) A WOMAN'S RIGHT TO CHOOSE?
4) THE RIGHTS OF MAN?
5) WHAT'S THE MEANING OF IT ALL?

LIKE AS LOVERS? WHY, NOONE RECOVERS FROM A RELATIONSHIP WITH THEM

ANSWERS!
1) THEY ENFORCE IT! 2) THEY DONT DISCRIMINATE 3) WHY EXTERMINATE OF COURSE!
4) YEP— EXTERMINATE 5) YOU GUESSED IT

the WOrd

FET- "LOOKING AFTER CATS" by Brace

no contradictions in this religion! everything is true & one Word's

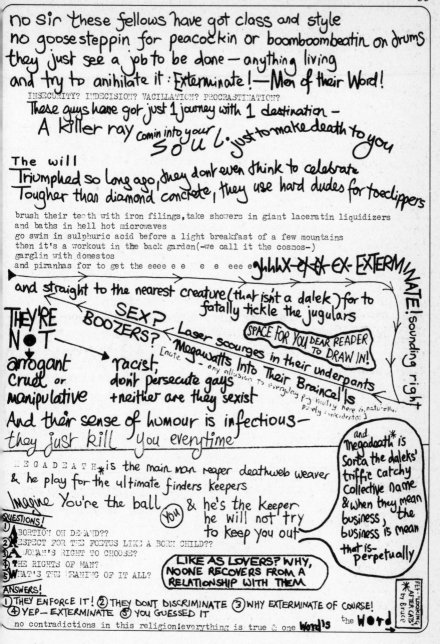

YOU ever had a feeling or a dream? These beauties want you to know
that they're trying to destroy it, aeons before you ever got/
even within maximum distance to it

it's nothing personal of course   nothing condescending
perfect desire   true love LLioN I .AYT YOUex-terrrmmmmmmmmina-te
well they're not really dying to - more determined than that- what they do to you/
                                                          they   just gotta get to you
Exterminate-ten out of ten owners say their lives get no choice in the matter
Exterminate-Vorsprung durch Endlösung, as they used to say in Germany

(daleks) | NOTE ————————

they're Not extremists
they're Moderates, easy goin
believe in free enterprise and
equal fair destruction for all.
these dudes know that killing
is just not cricket, and that
you don't shoot a man when
he's down. - you shoot him when
he's standing up just before

| Will the advert this refers to be shown /
remembered when the book I'm preparing this
piece for is published? Whatever, for those who
don't know German, this means : progress (with a
capital P) through (as in thanks to) the final
solution (i.e - in case some don't know - what the
Nazis called the institutionalized genocide they
orchestrated).
If this seems pedantic to anyone, you're probably
the kind of person who doesn't think to wanna
throw up on a writer when they throw in French
and Latin phrases with no translation.

to die is to be human — to massacre divine
you never see a dalek show off get boring or whine
You don't catch daleks hypocritically wingeing about genocide.

note - if you need a drink or a piss, we're not even halfway so this might
be a good moment to put the kettle on or whatever.

Y see daleks don't go in much for ʃ civil disobedience
        they don't take too kindly ʃ to militant inconvenience
have
You ever tried to shame a   dalek
by firing all your humanity outa both of your eyes?

SUDDENLY!!!!!!! when the daleks got loose, gandhi went gaga
and you better believe the daleks/didnt gone dada
just went on the rampage/sorta hootin/hell bent on their heaven
& you better be more scared than a grouse on august the eleventh

creatures of habit— methodical. meticulous.
not in the slightest incrementalist leastestest bit ridiculous
except when someone blows up one, exposin a stinky smokey
        jumped up dustbin, full of mangy wires an last year's
        technicolor yawn dumpling.
or   dr. shhhh-youknowwho- cracks a joke they don't get. like— any
                                                                    joKE→

:
Heard the one about the one legged dalek?
WE-AINT-GOT-NO-LEGS-WE'RE-TIN-TORSOES

Why did the dalek cross the road?
TO-EXTERMINATE-THE-OTHER-SIDE

How many daleks does it take to change a lightbulb?
ONE-EXTERMINATE

actually there is that they quite like tho they're not
one joke   sure why :

there was a caucasoid dalek   and the caucasoid dalek goes-"exterminate↓
              mongoloid dalek   and the mongoloid dalek goes-"exterminate↑
              negroid dalek   and the negroid dalek goes-"exterminate↓. get it?

and there is One Joke that they actually get! :

KNOCK KNOCK--who's there
EXTERMINATE--exterminate who?
EXTERMINATE¡EXTERMINATE¡EXTERMINATE¡EXTERMINATE¡EXTERMINATE¡EXTERMINATE¡EXTERMINATE

first page ran out on me. anyway.
second possible rule of poetry;
image/idea weaving, verbal
incontinence or whatever:
② GIVE US A
BREAK
WILL YA?

and a human spirit's right to choose
of the society for the protection of the unborn soul
this might be an announcement on behalf

what's the meaning of ↑ the silly lines? fuck all

now it's no use makin excuses or hangin out the garlics
gotta face up to the everywhere everpresent overkillin daleks
they got the biggest sense of history / the universe it aint
Big enough for them and the word mystery. one had to go &
it was just so no contest, anyone taking bets would have
EXPLODED —— infinity to one◆ and here's the twist /
so catch the gist / the daleks were invited by people like
you + me / to purge their hypertragic existences / of suffering
an misery ● and if to the daleks people could see no
alternative / it was as good as a blood scented blank cheque
open invitation. ■ these guys are real aliens / they don't take
no stock in immigration ⑥ and they'd blast the foundations
and the skyscrapers and the superstructure ≤ until
everywhere was love + peace + quiet + no more war—
just what so many / good people are fighting for
and in the cosmos you couldve heard a   thought drop
anyday of the week seem like a gutter spewing savage in greyday
                                                        rain
or the sunniest Superday in nirvana, according to your game➤

if you wanna pass on your problems to the next person
or let other people do your questioning for you
or keep yourself to yourself to yourself to yourself to yourself toyrs!
Consider Remembering:there's countless trigger orgasmic daleks out there
Who want the universe to roam,looking for someone like you,to murder and to maim.

dont you feel wanted?????

NOW WERE NOT STUPID
WE COULD CUT SOME
MEAN SPARKS SO SPIN
US YOUR VERSION OF
WHY SO MANY OF US

are wasting away our lives in glaring dark

now we're not stupid we
could cut some mean sparks
so tell spin us your
version o'why
so many of us are
wastingaway ourlives in
glaringdark & if

IF YOU SAY YOURE NOT
you   say   youre   not
HOW YOU GONNA PROVE

and you know I love to say it — prove it or lose it

howyougonnaprooooooooooooooooovitanyouknowilovetosayitproveitorloseit

YOURE A NEUTRAL?CONGRATULATIONS SIR!
RELEASE MORDOR-YOU JUST CALLED THE DALEKS
IT'S NOT YOUR JOB?COULDNT CARE LESS?
FREEFORM BABYLON-YOU'VE JUST WON
EVERYNIGHT'S STARPRIZE: COME ON DOWN!
PERMANENT AGONY UNDER THE DALEKS
DONT ASK ME?
FREEFORM OCEANIA EASTASIA AND EURASIA
WE GOT JUST THE WAY TO AGE YA
APOLITICAL?REALLY MADAM?
SO ARE THEY!
I'M SURE YOU'LL SEE EYE TO EYE

EXTERMINATE!
THAT'S THEIR CATCH PHRASE
THEY DONT NEED NO OTHER
WHEN IT COMES TO
RAPPIN+ HARDTALKIN THERE'S NO
TOUGHER

VIBRATO STACCATO ARMAGEDDONADO FUNK TO THE FINISH
AND HEDONIZING? LOOK—THESE GUYS GOT NO VICES
DONT KNOW WHAT SIN IS — THEY JUST
GET DOWN ▶

So the next time you walk into town
and on the dusty saloon filled mainstreet approaches you is a dalek
better think: do I go for my gun? Do you Feel Lucky Punk?...
(the sixth bullet is always evermeen in season)
or do I say < I got nothing to lose > + go volunteer
for the totalitarian legion

cos unless you make your own mind up
youre going oneway to hell
straightaway thattaway anyway
and that's one journey with nooooooooooooooooo
nadir climax finish
tomorrow now or yesterday.

Trust Everybody.......

HELL SWEET HELL and home is where the heart
HELL SWEET HELL is and destroyed will stay

..and dont let them out of your sight........

Exterminate—the Ultimate Argument
And something's gotta Win It.

Trust Everybody.And dont let them out of your sight.

LET'S·FINISH·WITH·A·WHODUNNIT·●●TO·PROVIDE·A·CUSHION·FOR·TO
DANGEROUS·LAND·ME ●●● WHO CREATED THE DALEKS ???
LET'S·PUT·THE·TURD·AMONG·THE·RATTLESNAKES·●●● ● ●
AND·SUSPECT·IT·WAS·POOR·OLD·GANDHI.

the moral? isnt one
the amoral?????????-an idiot's gotta do wotta idiot's gotta do
ʃ ɪɪɪɪɪɪɪɪɪɪɪɪɪɪɪɪɪɪɪɪɪɪɪɪɪɪɪɪɪɪɪɪ ɪɪɪɪɪɪɪɪɪɪɪɪ ʇǝssǝɔɔǝu ʇou ʇnq

will the eagles
devour
the angels?

and God said "Let there be Light" and....
Well we're... working on it Lord
an while we're on the subject — how did you get up there????

IF YOU WANT
A VISION
OF THE FUTURE
IMAGINE
A HUMAN FACE
...The End/ ...The Beginning..

LAUGHING. AT A JACKBOOT.   FOREVER.

Smithed by GANDHI VERSUS THE DALEKS © 1985 ↑ ↑ ↑ ↑ ↑ ↑ ↑ ↑ ↑ ↑ ↑ ↑

the radio waves and the record collections are full of men pleading
for women to come back to them / or else exhorting
women to make love with them. / or strutting round like beheaded cocks
maintaining that they never needed them in the first place.........
me? I'm laughing boy.

←GANDHI VERSUS THE DALEKS 1982

↑THAT'LL TORCH YA↑

GEOFFREY GODBERT

Scientology

I am in an unacceptable state
(as opposed to a desirable one).
An established member of the *Standard*
Oxford Capacity Analysis team
asked me to answer 200 questions
(including: 'are you a slow eater?' and:
'when passing a beautiful child do you
avoid showing interest rather than
looking or smiling?' and: 'is your facial
expression varied rather than set?');
and my *Raw Scores*, SOCA decided, put me
BELOW THE BROKEN LINE – *Attention Urgent.*
This means I am unstable and depressed,
nervous, uncertain and inactive,
inhibited, irresponsible,
critical, *lacking in accord* and withdrawn.
If only I had had the time and money
to join, I could have become stable,
happy, composed, certain, active, *aggressive,*
responsible and *appreciative*;
and I could have been able correctly to
answer questions like: 'does *emotional*
music have *quite an effect* on you?' and
'would you *buy on credit* with the hope
that you can keep up the payments?' and: 'do you
often *sit and think* about death, sickness, pain
and sorrow?' and have no need for anything
more; need not wonder what to do next, or
ever worry that the questions might change,
nor the answers always be the same.

Others will fail the global TV parlour
game test; the recycled paper they use
will be stained with the graffiti of agonising
and their inquisitors will not even smell

the hatred on their breath or feel the spit
in their face tasting of the real thing
as they ask: 'are personal interests
unable to sway you from sound decisions?'
'do you often feel depressed?' 'do you smile much?'
'do you speak slowly?' 'does life seem worthwhile?'
and we answer: I do. I can. I am.

MICHÈLE ROBERTS

The Oyster Woman
in memoriam Helen Smith

the corpse filed away in a tin drawer
of the state brain resurrects
herself: a hiccup, a sour taste
on the legal tongue

the pathologist, the surgeon, the policeman, the coroner
chew over the meaning of *victim* of *innocence*
there is indignation, there is gnashing of teeth
analysis shows
there is genital injury, head abrasions
and bruises, which are consistent with rape

their lips kiss the book, will speak truth
her lips are sealed; who kissed
her lips, who tore them?

certainly she was born
and slapped, and breathed
possibly she was drunk
and slapped, and sobered
possibly she was hysterical
and slapped, and shut up
possibly she indulged in sexual horseplay
and slapped his face, certainly she died

analysis shows
the woman on the couch is hysterical
she cries: I am dismembered
I am pulled apart by guilt and knowledge
I cannot remember anything about it
I cannot bear to, I cannot bear witness
I have taken leave of all my senses, I was not there
I shall cover my face

the daughter under the sheet
on the mortuary slab
is vowed to chastity and silence
the mother on the marble mattress in church
has lost her daughter, and has died in childbed
their shrouds, their wedding veils dissolve
into the salt swaddling bands of the sea

deep buried, the oyster sits
on the gravel bed men have dug for her
their fingers fret at her frilled
stone petticoats: they wish to culture her
her valves open in welcome; they insert grit
her valves close; our mouths bleed, and are full of rocks

the woman on the couch goes home
and reads the morning papers
in bed, the cave of her becoming
rolling her tongue over jagged words
she remembers the sea, her mother
she re-members herself, she is forced to become a poet
she is forced to bear witness, to defend herself
then from the injuries inflicted she creates pearls
investigation shows
the details of the injuries inflicted
were omitted at the first hearing
the decision to omit them had been taken
in order not to distress her father
because they were not relevant

knowledge of the body is not relevant
but the body resurrects itself, and returns
home in a tin boat, borne across the sea
which stutters over and over
at jagged logical rocks
which interrupts the chatter of death
sentences with staccato pearls

at the first hearing of our words
our willingness to admit inside knowledge
to admit that we were there, that we were witnesses
that we could speak of it, caused much distress

the woman on the couch is much distressed
in order that the fathers may not be distressed

in order that
the pathologist, the surgeon, the policeman, the coroner
may have clean hands, may return home
to lie
between clean sheets, to dream of clean
daughters and filthy whores

CHRIS CARDALE

One foot

I have a lot to say,
a lot to do,
before I slip up
in the blood on the streets,
spilled by the mad doctors,
dissecting each other
to find the root of their skin difference.
all they find is hearts the same,
livers, kidneys, bladders, bones and lungs the same,
and in anger they throw them in our faces,
and in stupidity they worry at the back passages of the brain

with calipers and rules,
and the measured pieces being no good
for their absurd purposes,
they measure more and more,
and nothing on the human scale.

but before it all gets too bloody,
this is what I'd like to say:
I walk down the road, one foot, one foot.
I knock on one door then another,
one door, one door,
and everything is controlled, the feet,
and the food to fuel the feet, and the fist
on the door on its handle opening it,
and I wonder is this person on the other side
prepared for the unexpected visitor,
because I am always uninvited,
because nobody knows who I am.
nobody knows what I'd be like if I let go.
I don't know what I'd be like if I let go,
but I believe it would be good,
one good, one good, but I don't know,
and I watch out for raised eyebrows,
for that could be fear of what I do,
and I watch out for lowered eyebrows,
for that could be to block out my light,
to only see one thing not my thing.

I walk down the road, one foot, one foot,
one foot.
I knock on one door, then another,
one door, one door, one door,
and I'm looking for something inside me
outside me, so I know I can totally let go,
and I talk, and I shout, and I scream loud,
and I run, and this is close, and I dance,
and this is closer still, and I make love,
and this is closest of all, but always
there is more, every item of control

in a piece of music tells me
there is more, there is a lightness of touch,
a quickness of movement with purpose,
to show me there's more to letting go
than I could have descried in me so far,
though my body shakes, trembles and vibrates
though my hair stands on end and my spine becomes a cool river –
I notice children climbing from high places
with a purpose that forgets legs and arms
which follow rapidly and gracefully, their control is letting go.

I walk down the road, one foot, one foot,
one foot, one foot.
I knock on one door, then another,
one door, one door, one door, one door,
and there are police – symbols of control –
and there is a time for getting to work,
and schedules to keep, meetings to make,
eight hours sleep, at least one meal a day,
money to make, bodies to wash, for what?

the only good reason for control is to let it go
to find out what being totally human is,
to find out what to be immeasurable is,
to find out what the going rate for life is,
to find out all the ways of saying hullo,
to find out all the things this body's for,
why I dream of soaring and not being alone,
why I dream at all, to smash my hourly price,
to live in one priceless human moment,
one of a string that all of u are in,
to shatter the concepts of debt and payment,
I believe that love is simply going first
and the only good reason for control is to let it go.

I walk down the road, one foot, one foot,
one foot, one foot, one foot,
I knock on one door, then another,
one door, one door, one door, one door, one door.

DESMOND JOHNSON

Ole Charlie Boy

Ole charlie boy
you still deh a inglan
charlie boy
you still deh a london
yes
   mi sey
      mi sey
         mi sey
            mi sey
yes
   mi sey
      mi sey
         mi sey
            mi sey
razing mi voice a likkle
e did fass
fe ask mi dat question
cause we both is in
de same position
for we both come
here in de fifties
a kinda runaway
from yard perplexities
an we all come find
de same sin-ting
low paid jobs
bad housing
so yes
   mi sey
      mi sey
         mi sey
            mi sey

yes
 mi sey
  mi sey
   mi sey
    mi sey
mi still on de dole
still in de hole
still is as bruck
and can't find no wok
what about your children
charlie boy
what about you plan dem
charlie boy
well
 mi sey
  mi sey
   mi sey
    mi sey
well
 mi sey
  mi sey
   mi sey
    mi sey
mi only boy is as worser than mi
dem sen him to prison
on dem new sus law
dem sen him to prison
cause dem catch him with a draw
and de gals dem a breeding agen
dem total children come to ten
de mada an mi is not so sweet
she sey all mi do is to walk de street
ole johnny boy
 time is rough
  ole johnny boy
   time is tough
mi save up so money
mi waa fe go home

telephone de airport people dem
ole johnny boy
   time is rough
     ole johnny boy
       time is tough
de cost fe de flight
is more dan wha mi have
coulda sell de house
if belong to mi
old johnny boy
   time is rough
     ole johnny boy
       time is tough
mi ago die in inglan
johnny boy
we ago die in inglan
johnny boy
cause mi bruck in inglan
johnny boy
cause we bruck in inglan
johnny boy
ole johnny boy
   time is rough
     ole johnny boy
       time is tough!

JAMES BERRY

In the loneliness of a tramp

Don't I walk a nomad about the city?
Don't I carry ragged gestures
I keep as mine, in bagfuls
of questionmarks: who am I? Who?

Where are the wise people
to come out many-sided like trees

and not symmetrical like rooms, not
copies of winners with certain voices,
and not be a glamour-nothing like me,
this audience of one,
a companion without company?

Peculiar this, said so before:
queer bundles hooked on asking,
who speaks for me. Who then I say,
who farts on diet of scraps
from Temple to the Middlesex?
Who repeats that seeing of shooting
stars, and that icy rat-nibble on his
genitals, raising alarm in newspaper
bedding? Who I say, who can't elect
himself into a post of MP?

All this dirt I'm under is mine:
no more than smells like an ancient king.
But who knows my difference makes
non-difference? Everybody knows
my stillborn deaths are all unburied.
Who knows I can't clear what I left,
can't see mine I walk past?
Every bloody person just knows
and knows and knows I stink!

Who I say, who knows getting bloody warm
is work? Who knows keeping a bladder
topped up, and not pee, is a damn good game
that not every arse of a perfumed beard
can play? Where are the different eyes
on the road, carriers of youthful summers
that I for one would have no need
of meeting eyes that purr like a cat.

Who wants to look out from me,
to stand in chapped cold feet?
Always I've spent clean, yes, but I owe
not a Clever Dick one penny credit.

Never to beg, never to borrow, I say
always, seizing only what's left about.
Yet who knows my manifesto? Who knows
I have a ready TV speech and a Parliament
speech? Who knows nomad knowledge counts?

Going smeared and stained and stuck to,
own breath around crusty as spilt sauce
and semen, I have time my endless mantra
repeating open spaces and wheels
and feet passing. And my fellows'
heads go bald, banging
low ceilings of achievement.

I walk puzzled, yes I do,
at what touch wakes me each day
to the ugliness of my freedom.
Yet haven't I measured my distance,
well away from clever-clever vices?

DONAL CARROLL

Rum runner
'dress up and drop out' (*Style*)
Dick Hebdige

Wind-skint, they gird up their macho, wooing
in traditional style; strut, jut, linger
and strategic disinterest that would pull
success . . . anywhere else but here
where the event pours its insides out in
to the alley each time the door opens
showering them with sound and rising salsa:
the doorman fouls their eyes, ignoring them.

Inside, spaced in, the sound becomes a look;
in a petty-Borges atmosphere,
newage choirboys and matinee dreamboats

ignore teenage grannies who ignore twotones,
subalterns of style, ignoring the odd
couple, Eric Flynn and Rita Haywhat
ignoring Bog-art, salivating gum,
dressed in a conceptual mackintosh,
knocking back stacks of rock'n roll mouthwash
ignoring the spare Ted, well Lazarus'd.

Latin l'amours wear off the shoulder
highwaymen with Dick Turpintine cocktails,
pirates eye shadow Regency dandies
bockerknickered with brio and Brylcreem
and suffering from terminal flashback;
the ballet dressed talking bicep with the
authority of Sandra Dee's underwear
quotes a crinoline; cubby-hole peacocks.

The dearth of cocktail kitsch cruelty wear
goes unnoticed; the military fatigues;
Bowie clones invade the space placed round them,
wiggle their toggle, skeletal small-boying,
with their affliction curtaining one eye,
a hair so conscious, it speaks its own lines;
all electronicking about the floor,
they salon, with a chip in their shoulders,
micro-moving the process of dancing:
even a fractured eyelash is action.

This is the world of protective clothing;
style whiles away the climate of doing,
of necessity, other than itself;
sobbing soubrettes sartorial stimulants –
the socially biodegradable;
suddenly 'Tomorrow belongs to me'
appears, a brown-shirted moment-ignored
like the price of the beer in the hunt for
the glint round the necklace of Narcissus.

PAUL A. GREEN

Directions to the dead end

1

Be prudent:
This planet has a beginning,
a middle and an end,
At the dead end, dismount.
Walk through the burying ground, touch
the mound
at the base.
Look up at the tower, the grid,
the silvery, hairy antennae.
Watch the panel on the plinth,
the dials, the frozen meters, the icicle spiders
reach solid state.
The absolute is zero.
Perfect machines contain no moving parts.

2

Do not panic, do not be pagan. Be prudent. Avoid convul-
sions. Hear these instructions. You must not forget you
are approaching the dead end. There will be no more signals. Follow our signs. The handrails are provided for
your own protection. Remain on the path. *Avoid spoors.*
Do not be disturbed by our guides. They are there to help
you, across the final metres of the midnight zone. *Abstain
from beans.* Do not remove your masks. The guides will
intone your name when the time comes. Do not remove your
gloves. They will be specially treated for the final
handshake. *Do not expose yourselves.* Do not accept any
immodest songs, books, or pictures that might be offered
to you at the wayside. *Protect your nervous system.* At
the dead end, on the ledge of the dead end,

STAND BACK

The slim end of the shining edge is hardened, serrated, *live.*

3
I arrived at the dead end several days ago
after many evolutions
after ritual purifications
after stamping out my birthmark
after slicing out my tumours
after exorcising my spasms
after smoking out my nest of serpents
after hammering my shadow
after burning down my statues
after cutting up my writing
after breaking my assemblies
after erasing my warped tapes
after distilling my bodily fluids
after savaging my dogs
after draining off my cesspit and smashing the sump
after smashing my crutch and cane
after scouring my fleshpots
after strafing my floodlit bed
after testing my gold guardians (chuckling in sulphuric acid)
after tickling my clown to death
after strangling my private puppet
after stuffing my corpses with fuel-soaked rags
after digging my own cave
after flooding my charred ark
after the purgative flood
after human sacrifice

I came to the dead end
3000 light years from the Vatican
where all the parallels converge.

4
Infinity is dotted with rotating corpses . . .
their domed helmets sparkle, their tangled life-lines
unroll from concave bellies
and particles of an enormous query
jerk through their barbed electric fibres

The transmitter floats a few feet away
from the rim of the dead end.
It is spherical, compact, and far too small.

BILL GRIFFITHS

Found texts on birds

(has nested) (has bred) (not white) (not yellow) (has bred) (mainly Nor-
folk) (unlike Song Thrush) (not illustrated) (not screaming) (has bred)
(not barred) (nest-boxes) (not slate-blue as Peregrine) (slightly tap-
ered) (breeds in Wales) (male) (very few) (breeds locally) (male) (female)
(juvenile Plovers easily confused) (has bred) (no white spots) (not
brown)

residents summer-visitors migrants vagrants in kettles walls paper
gorse in a lined and decorated cup in letter-boxes ledges herbage
burrows buildings gulleries

Eggs on Plates IX–XII greenish-grey bluish-white (goldfinch) green-
ish-blue (redstart) reddish-brown (greenfinch) greyish-mauve yell-
owish-white greenish-white (blackbird) greyish-white (yellow-ham-
mer) bluish-grey olive-brown brownish-white creamy-white bluish-
green lilac-grey pale-greenish-blue pale-bluish-green creamy-yell-
ow yellowish-brown greyish-blue yellowish-grey glossy-white

pica-pica picus-canus pintail pipit-meadow pipit-red-throat' pipit-
richard's pipit-rock pipit-tawny pipit-tree pipit-water godwit-bar-
tail godwit-black-tail knot guillemot gull-common gull-herring gull-
little gull-ross's risca robin roller rook ruff YELLOW . . HAMMER
hoopoe

MAUREEN DUFFY

Chattel

Driving back from the literature festival
through Otley handsome in black stone
with white revers of painted windows and doors
I follow behind a tin truck
gaping an open vent high up at the back.
Stopped at the lights the gap is filled
with broad snout, a wet black sponge for sucking up
sweetness from deep in summer grass.
You crane your head in the hole sideways to let
each eye in turn roll up at the sky.
Deep in tumbril shock you don't speak.
I know where you're going this summer's morning
and feel you know it too though how
when no one has ever come back with telltale
smell of blood and fear on staring hide?
I imagine though I can't see the shrunken dug
flat as a perished rubber glove.
The street is called Wharfedale View. It looks across
to where the moors throw a green quilt
for miles under a high sky. Why can't I just
draw the steel bolt on the tailgate
and let you run up there till you drop?
But the lights change. You turn Left; I go Right
for Leeds and perhaps I'm quite wrong
and you're just being moved on to new pasture.
Then why can't I safe home sleep
but still see your face laid along the tailgate
with one moist eye turned up questioning
whether I would have drawn that bolt
if you'd been able to ask me in a tongue
I couldn't kid myself I misunderstood.

FREDERICK WILLIAMS

Storm

Wen storm com
Storm noh form de fool
Im huff an jus puff
An she jus flatten every ting

Warna Marie pass trough an a warn
Beware – Beware, distruction is near
Rain – Lightenin – Tunda
Wind and rain floods upon floods
River ah goh com dung bank to bank

Nail up yuh winda an yuh doors
Lock up yuh cow, goat, horse,
Pigs, foul, donkey and mule
De wise wi listen to dis warnin
De fool wi wate till its too late

Wen storn com
Storm rip off sheet ah zinc
Off ah smaddy house
Zinc fly an chap mi in mi head
For mi one little two room wattle an dawb
Gone ah sea

Wen storm com
Tables tun – right, left, up side dung
Twist – bend – bruck up in pieces
Storm blow dung house, kill ratta, kill mouse
Banana tree blown dung
Coconut tree, breadfruit tree
Mango tree, blown dung

De grung covah wid green mango
Ripe mango, young mango
Whole heep a fruits well washed
Som broken, som mashed

Wen storm com
Who use to have, noh have noh more
Who nevah have got too much
Whole heep a ave am, ave am noh want am
Whole heep ah want am, want am caan get am

Friends – neighbours – an relations
Ah run from yard to yard
From districk to districk
Fe se if everyone arite
Is de sam ting I wus doin
In de middle ah de nite
Wen zinc fly an mi nearly loose mi head

Wen storm com
Gully com dung bank to bank
Calbut caan teck watah
Watah wash ova eena road
Yuh haffe good fe cross de ford

Wen storm com
Storm noh fear no foe
Storm jus give woe
For Warna Marie did com warn
Bout de lightenin an tunda
Brimstone and Fire
Wat ah woe

Storm wreck car, truck, bus
Storm bruck dung bridge an buildin
Weh no even dun meck
Storm teck up house lan it pon river
House tun boat

Mi noh like wen storm com
Storm play havok pon man, woman an chile
An wile all dat ah gwaan
Nuff baby a bawn
Dem name dem storm babies
Janet, David, Betsy

Storm completely rearrange de environment
Den de Government
Handin out provisions
Of second an third han clothin
Little milk, little flour, rice, sugar
Piece ah cheese fe tease yuh appetite
Little kerosene oil fe light de nite
An de fight to survive
Jus change gear in de eight month of de year

Storm skips ova rivers an dances o'er de seas
Dippin an risin, dippin an risin
Leavin behine a pitch black horror show on lan
Ah man wen day light
I taught I wus havin a dream
Lastin ten long nites
Den de sun came up
An de prayers went up
Takin Jah for bein alive

Compare storm to a Yankee invasion if yuh like

But Darlin wen your love came
T'was just like a storm

III

NO COMMON GROUND

MAHMOOD JAMAL

Sugar-coated pill

A clever adversary
does not advertise his intentions.
He will come with a big smile
to show his love; and slogans
that even you would hesitate to shout.
Freedom, Peace and Equality
will never be far from his lips
and he will offer every help
to keep you where you are.
A split soul, a lost language
the poison of gifts
the symptoms of slow penetration.
Fantasies on the screen,
arguments that are 'self evident'
And you feel a romantic fool
for trying to change the world.
'Be my wife, my child
and all shall be well.'
Flowers, chocolates, perfumes, gadgets
his subtle armaments; what else
could you ask for
being hopelessly divided
friendless, faceless, full of fears.
And while you man the barricades
in battledress keeping an eye out for
intruders,
He surprises you with an embrace.
You have been disarmed!

H. O. NAZARETH

The Promised Land

The people keep dying.
Their ancient cradle of faiths
and blood-letting still devises
new forms of dying
to try out on them.

They keep dying
like houses falling,
like hearts failing,
like storm-wrecked palms,
like a watch on the wrist of a child with no arms.

Feuding nomads, catacomb Christians,
dispersed Jews, Muslims with no East to turn to –
their intimacy with suffering grew
within cultures devoted to
both sense and sensuality
that dramatises every bit of dying they now do.

Lobo sees it as a kind of immortality sustained
by imperial powers from Egypt and Rome
through to modern ones. Now the home-
land is a ball and chain
fixed to ankles forced to linger elsewhere,
overrun by strangers who have come
to call it exclusively their dom-
ain at the expense of many of its people who remain.

The people keep dying.
Who can say they'll gain
the promised land,
settle down to life and death
like most other human beings –
and forfeit their poisoned immortality?

JACKIE KAY

Prizes

Princess Anne was on the telly
last night she got the woman
of the year human-itarian award
and I thought My God she can
jet-set to famine across
continents flying with her
arrogance and jewels and
her own bunch of servants
on working people's money
and she gets an award for that!

She said she had some unfinished
business in India, that she'd been
to Ethiopia she said Ethiopia has
Problems not only the lack of
water and food but the culture
and religion I might have known
she'd say they were starving
because they are heathens –

I saw a thousand missionaries stand behind
her bringing a White God to the mouths of
the swollen-bellied children a White God
to feed them loaves, fishes and a hard book
white is good and Judas was a Black man
and your dance is the dance of the Devil.

Princess Anne was on the telly last night
England has not changed.
The coloniser still constant in the vowel I
the Imperialist wish, the unfinished business
the wish travels from India to Kenya
from Nigeria to Hong Kong
England still gives prizes
to princesses who preach
the New Missionary Tongue

in the tone of a Memsahib
the old slaveholder philosophy
and she wants to call this Aid?

Tell me. Is it humane that this
woman should be dripping with
wealth whilst the black children's
bellies bulge as one mother
after another's eyes widen
in grief and disbelief
as another child dies
as another child dies
as insects feast on their heads
England, this England gives
standing ovations to a Princess
who rides horses over black
people's dreams and they say
this is humanitarian
this is humane.

BARBARA BURFORD

Empire

Windsong, windbells
and a mountain.
The green echo.
These are my morning.

The blue hum of wasps
in the Lignum Vitae.
The tang of silver polish,
and twenty lamps to fill.
These are my forenoon.

Ripe cucumber, sea salt, pepper.
Sun-bleached linen,
the river bend where the mermaid lives.

A dragonfly.
These are my afternoon.

The moon flirting
behind a palm-leaf fan.
The Ladies dance
the quadrille in white.
No knives left in the cookhouse:
this will be our night.

MAHMOOD JAMAL

Silence

Let my silence speak out
through these words.
Let it seep through these sounds
imperceptibly
as the air we breathe
permeates our blood.

Let the silence
grow as the words grow denser
thickets, bushes, thorny branches
standing in a windless evening;
silent
brooding darkly of day
passing shadow-like
into the dark.

The silence of deep deserted
eyes
    and pitch black
tears.
The silence of moonlight
over the shanty towns.
The silence
inside a gun's mouth
when the bullet has flown.

The silence
of a child's twisted belly
and his old eyes.

Let my silence speak
as the eloquent silence
of lovers;
the silence of clouds passing
and black evening hills;
the silence of dew damply
falling over graves.
So the silence
can grow as the noise grows
about us of robots
and demogogic lights
that shriek out on the desolate highways
their neon screams.

So that the dark
can be discovered
So that the silenced
are not forgotten
Let my silence be loud.

KEITH JEFFERSON

Canto Africanus erectus
For Paul Robeson, Walt Whitman and the Last Poets

Come all swank villagers
Who are dwarfed by this night;
Round-backed from the bulk of that Negress
Ladling her luminous orb of chalk

Come all rain-soaked walkers
Sighting from your line of huts
A great indigo whale
With its solitary barnacle of light.

Come at the swelling peal of my bell
This cracked and mossy American thing
O come to this black barn
Come with your sack of bread and Dago accents
Come with your pumpkins, squash
Come from the lip of an answerable thing
The green breath seen in the bite of Fall
The line of the hawk calling . . .

O come from the North

    with the man whose ax sweats
    by the side of his bed,
    who covets a mirror of himself from the Sun
    who longs like a squaw
    for his own hot light

O come from the South

    with the bow-legged gal whose dog
    paces the yardgrass to dust
    whose swarthy skin is the tint of her pack
    who moans in the humidity of sea swells
    as the screen door bangs like an old wooden heart

O come from the West

    with the hundred yawning survivors
    of the Lusitania: hair braided and shining
    the truth of Poseidon distorting their ears
    to wings: let us now deliver the war
    they were promised

O come from the East

    where rovers have been awakened
    and oil themselves with the wax of elms
    whose boots are wormy with rot.
    Can you hear their shrill girl-like voices
    mimicking piccolos and fifes
    those cool tin cones from the
    Spanish Civil War? Can you hear them, señor?

All you simple sons of Guernica, of Selma
I plan to catch the iron horse to town
I plan to disrupt whatever hangings there be
I plan a camp with all the cast-off world niggers
    with their rosesilk cards and gypsy numbers
    booty swapped beneath the pock-marked moon

All you sturdy daughters of Ho Chi Minh City, Trenchtown and
    Harlem

Here's to the horse of Tecumseh
Here's to the breakneck speed of the Underground railroad
Here's to a rent party on the back of Venus
O this Sunday tent of religion
Has housed my 99 screams

One third of fear, one third of desire
One third to be filled by the squirming bastard
Of the two
Of which the deep voice of the One sirens

Of which the deep blue voice of the One
Cautions to watch the minute mathematics of the clouds
To believe achingly in the mystery of wheat
To trust the library of the Body
To be always and always kind
To be always and always moveable

Now the crows and hummingbirds see my spell
Big eyes for the reading, monster alphabets
Calling
This heart asks for asylum
And it is to those hot borders I go

This heart asks for asylum
And it is to those hot borders I go
With my wick of bread burning in this belly of ancestors
The song of old Africanus erectus
10,000 faces spiralling like geniis

10,000 dreams oozing from the seams of my spine
       pooling in my tap-tap feet
       shuffling to my own chattering snare
10,000 voices, multi-layered
       an extra in 'Green Pastures', choiring for De Lawd
       warbling bout de firmament dat we all love
10,000 feet, pacing the bowl of my gut
       that flesh that speaks
       that flesh that cajoles the Flat Earthists
       this gut that throws stones at your dragons
         of steam
       that scapegoat lizard murmuring Islam
       at the edge of Europe

This heart asks for asylum
And it is to those hot borders I go
For those who will not leave
       who will stay for 12 tedious seasons
       who will dress a nightmare in wool
       who are violent in their refusal to dream out loud
       who celebrate their skeletons from dance

O the wick of bread in my belly burns!
O the wick of bread in my belly burns!
O there is a coming in the barn
For here is the manger-birth of action!
For here we save the tiny worlds that feed us!

This noisy heart screams for asylum!
Calls for the increase crowd
The swell-march to the forest
The meeting at midnight near the den of foxes
The rimshot cracking of dry, dry Manzanita

O the wick of bread in my belly burns
For the smouldering churches of the mind
For the carried ashes and the ash of the face
For the weeping rocks and the secret cabbages
For the river that swells from the weight
  of black children

From black children's weight the veins of
   this land shall pus and burst,
For the river that courses through these
Negro sad eyes
O a wick of bread in my belly burns

And I beat the belly chant for the holy sufferers
Striking the bell with the thick of my arm
Come villagers and hoist me
To the crest of the barn
Where my red can be sensed
Where my thirsty bark can glint its teeth
And tick with the blood of the asylummed heart

I strike the bell cast
From the heart of a witch
For the man whose head was etched by a child
For the slower ones, the misunderstoods
The stuttering nuns that cackle in the alcove

I strike the bell cast
From the bone of a giant
For those imprisoned for stabbing the lie
For he who upsets the tray of the severed head
For the breathing talkers clouding our winters with warmth
For the lovers of crimson, speed and guffaws
For the friends of Nijinsky in his piss-stained cell
For the friends of Robeson who sang death and hate to sleep

I strike the bell cast
From the syrup of gold
I strike the bell cast
From the skulls of my family, my gracious hosts of Sienna
I strike the bell cast
From the sigh of the sunset
From the deep coloured tears of Sadness, Belief and Wonder
From the inestimable breadth of hands
I strike the bell cast
From my own romantic leaving

This ringing measures
In the star-belched tempo of night
My own fresh longing

And all the tireless steps
Towards my
Eventual return

JOHN AGARD

First black man in space

Afro-Cuban cosmonaut, 38-year-old Arnaldo Tamayo Mendez, became the
first black man in space as part of the two-man crew of the USSR space
craft, SOYUZ 38. (From a news release in *Caribbean Contact* October 1980.)

Others before him had gone
and come back
with their token
of moonrock
had planted their flag
and spoken
of the absence of gravity
the lightness of the body
that strange-dimensional sensation
of a spacesuit foetus
floating on moondust
a goldfish capsuled
in a galactic aquarium
with possible pebbles of uranium

But no one had prepared him for this
the booklets and leaflets
had said nothing of this
No the intensive briefing
had not prepared him for a meeting
with God face to face.
The press had hailed him
a national hero

an honour to the nation
a first for his race
a revolutionary breakthrough
but of this not a single clue.
Nothing about meeting
with God face to face
in outer space

Not one word
that God would be black
moreso a woman
and would greet him
not with a coke and hamburger
saying 'Geewhizz guy you made it'
but would embrace him
as a long-lost brother
of her race
would utter his name
offering him a cup
of maté tea
after the long journey
would say 'Compañero
a la luna bienvenido'

Wait till this gets back
to Moscow
or worse still Cape Canaveral

They won't believe the satellite photo
this will be a blow
for space exploration

NICKI JACKOWSKA

Africas

This doll beats his drum.
If this doll came of grass he would
tramp the field down.
But he is root-crop, blade-hidden.

If this doll asks, how shall I answer?
He makes time curl out of his belly
like a dark snake.

If I ask this doll, how is his tongue made
will it have time to spell the hours of
his dancing, before the scythe dips.
Which time will he choose for his saying.

This doll beats her drum,
the sound is locked in.
Shall I ask of her land a different
colour, a basin of dreams.

She thrusts out her breasts and speaks.
How are they carved, parted across
the table, how are they twin.

FREDERICK WILLIAMS

More space

Every day mi wake
Mi haffe seh
But for Jah-Jah sake
Wah gwaan

De reason and de passion clash
A fight one anedda fe de right
To smash down forces
Dat suppresses me
An impede me progress

Now afta many, many
Frustrated moments
Reason an passion
Join as one an decide
Sweat fe sweat
Blood fe blood

Kind words cant full belly
Promise cant meck bed
Hail de new diplomacy

An dont tell mi
Dat a talk too much
Bout Africa an race

These are ever burnin issues
Yu want fe sweep unda de carpet

Yuh betta yu hav carpet
I dont even hav sleepin space
Jah knows dat my race
Needs more SPACE

Space fe live an gi wi pickney
De lickle comfat
Space fe spread out not fe show off
Like hebby cuttin pon nuttin
But fe show off de talent weh wi got

Giv us more space
Meck wi show wi face pon telly
Meck wi hear wi voice via wireless

Wi want space fe do wi ting
Fe play wi music an sing

Why should one race
Run all ova de place
Occupying all de space

Mansion yaso empty
Palace deso empty
Castle yaso empty
Stately home deso empty

An if yu squat
Dem skin up dem face
De shout wat, get de law
Trow dem squatters out

De only space wi get in de popular media
Is to portray stereo type an degredation

Draw back draw back
Gimi some space
SPACE yes SPACE

Dressback man
A want som space
Where a can jump back
Rock an swing mi han

Dem dont giv us any option
Dem seh all who beg not gettin
An who dont beg dont want
An yu cant jus teck
Dem wi call yuh tief
So wi will haffe start capture

JEREMY SILVER

Different histories

My history is different from yours
my family line perhaps resplendent or exotic
as the least of them

A spectre behind Europe
I can not discover
we were plundered and in disarray
herded then gassed like animals
and who can say now
where we came from except from Aharon
from officers at the Temple

Recent past agonies
are blue numbers deep in the skin
scarred minds palaces of loss
built upon loss all

left behind before I was born the mud tracks
of the *Stetl* they had their grooves and ruts
outlined sharply by the moon
the wooden houses breathed noiselessly
breath from which I come

Connections only made in the hook of my nose
high cheeks cut against the howling
I scarcely know where to look in this frustrate
dream but I have been in these northerly places
Auschwitz Treblinka Buchenwald
the stately names shoulder me
cut in the curve of my spine

As border-light between thin reeds of darkness
the people we came out of our houses
to leave before dawn this is my family
I cannot know my family line
with carts and bundles my family line

The long track that goes away a felled tree
its many twigs branches already aflame
and one bough still sappy reaches forward
into this waking world this luxury
of assimilation and quiet nights

All that kept me together all
the difference is diminished
and diminishes me
this history is different from yours
how roughly similar we pretend to be.

GRACE NICHOLS

Tapestry

The long line of blood
and family ties

an African countenance here

a European countenance there
an Amerindian cast of cheek
an Oriental turn of eye
and the tongue's salty accommodation
the tapestry is mine
all the bloodstained prints
the scatterlinks
the grafting strand of crinkled hair
the black persistent blooming

LINDSAY MACRAE

For Michael Smith who is dead

Colour isn't something
we are taught to love.
When we were bald and blind,
bundles of pinky flush;
gawping and sent to relatives
with letters:
'Healthy, little perfect eight pound girl –
looks like her dad'
You were arriving labelled
and welcome to the dirty work.
And we had milky dreams.
And we had seaside holidays
where every face was white
Soon it got around
– the hand in front of mouth –
that someone black
had simply been
in the sun too long.

I have been speaking
out of a skin
which passed the window test
We have been hiding in our carelessness.
There is no common ground

or shared experience,
though some of us pretend.
You were the gentlest of men
to call me sister.

PENELOPE TOFF

Serenade
For Hazel

Serenade in the Night was performed in London in July 1985.
It tells the story of a coloured woman living under Apartheid.

A state of emergency
is declared

South Africa
state of power

and you dance
declaration of intent
you are screaming
that death stands
at every door
still standing

so you tear
its heart out
stop my pulse with
each twist and curve

power of body
power of mind

the sponsor refused to see
wanted his bed
and his safe white woman
who does not tear
the morning paper with her teeth
smash the silent marmalade

he says
if you will not
perform for him
then no one else
shall hear

says it's not 'art'
when the fear
licks at your ears
not theatre when the anger
lands in your lap
follows you home

taste the dust
the hard rain

rivers of mud and salt flow
at KwaThema and Springs
today
open your doors
but shut your mouth
bleed in silence today

make the most of it Botha
let your statement
echo
while we bury our dead

before me
this woman
is outdancing death

i bring to her a soft rain
she kisses me with fire

in South Africa
erupts   a
volcano

HERETIC WOMEN

ALISON FELL

Fantasia for Mary Wollstonecraft

There's the same view:
mottled trees, the squat chapel;
the boys on the spring streets
still raucous and glossed as
blackbirds, yodelling out
for just anybody, and oh
breakneck Mary how we go round
on the great wheel of April,
to be tugged or broken, pushed out
still streaked and yolked, our skin
transparent to the blood

You're here, old bully at my right
ear, storming radically up
to a broken blue place where
girls will grow
unimaginably into themselves
Your pen leaps across this blown
and blinding day in the city;
And the dream is
to be afraid of nothing
and dare everything – horses,
defeats, vendettas – to act
with a raw edge

Or else you go hungry, and your thoughts
are the colour of spiders –
that tittering in the distance,
this drab woman with her
schoolmistressy smile, does she
presume? He's with that actress
again, that pepper-and-salt
rouge-pot, everybody knows it;
but you don't pine when your mind
is a knife to slice with

Into the river, then, on
an oily night without stars
Under the spars of the bridge your
stupid hem bloating up, blundering
yards of petticoats floating you,
and even your dense energy won't
take you down

Indestructible Mary, how you
sigh on your dry beach, the days
sit in your mouth like stones
Saying you stay alive only
for superior tasks – all your
frippery sisters just asking to be
put in order, and ardent France, too,
tearing at you like a red trumpet

You want fresh strength,
possibilities of men and mercy
and to give and give, to see love
and revel in the rights and wrongs
of it, to look it in the teeth
(no masks, now or ever)

Timid Godwin trembles at
your relish – all this
under the woman's skirts, desire
silver down her spine, and
doesn't she dance on his wounds,
teasing and smirking?

The quarrels raking you together,
a stubborn gathering of two
donkeys thinking freely and
biting each other, so who
the devil would believe he'd
turn husbandly and you
hold still and temper
for the child's sake

Mooning Mary on a winning
streak, this next birth
will be different
September-smoky and encircled
by love, it will be fierce fruit,
a gay deliverance. It will
give you Godwin, too, irreversibly
(this day with the name
of your real death)

Modern Mary you have
travelled and arrived, yet in
the heat of the heart of it,
a terrible fever pins you to yourself
Such ravishing cold – nothing
was ever meant to be like this

Blackbirds' wings like a sudden fast scratching
and even as you shake your life out
they are using you singularly
to stifle their girls – oh shocking

Mary, you strumpet   you
plural woman   you plainest prophet

DEBORAH LEVY

Red Rosa
For Rosa Luxemburg

So Rosa wrote letters
to her lover
whose revolutionary
ardour   renounced
touch
when she most needed
touch   Rosa

on platforms
smashing the rotten
globe,   Berlin's
hard testicle   Rosa

in factories
feeding torn hearts
strategy   Rosa

yellow star
unties her Polish hair
wants to overcome   Rosa

red star
lifts up her skirts
scans her belly   Rosa

bright star
wants to love
tonight.   Tomorrow

they club her
to death.   Imagination
to death.   Rosa

often heretics
are better off dead.
Often heretic women
die celibate.   Burying
the fleshy debate.

VALERIE SINASON

My mother, burning

My mother, the fire queen
grows volcanoes in her window-box.
We do not have a garden.

I am pointing to the flowers on the mantelpiece
that smoulder in their blackened vase.

'Such a lovely smell,' says mother,
her bonfire eyes lighting.

My mother, the fire-raiser,
opens the petrol can of her mouth.
She is singing me a nursery rhyme.
Her words crackle into smoke.

A flame is tearing down the smooth skin
of her right arm.
She is still singing.
She cannot see she is burning.

My mother, burning,
I am trying to keep wet for her.
I am trying to keep us safe.

I buy her cream for her skin,
gauze and liniment,
oven gloves and safety scissors.
I promise her
a fire extinguisher of tears.

My mother, burning,
hungry for coal, wood,
my matchstick arms and legs.

I soak in the sea all day
but she surfaces in tidal waves,
her bushfire hair running near.
Nothing stops her from burning.
No sea can make her wet.

Mother, how can I stop you
burning our joint skin?
The scar on your arm
runs through my veins.

I live with a fire detector,
an electric oven.
I do not strike matches, light fires,
burn leaves.

But inside me the smoke rises
from your poor burnt flesh
and I worry if I have enough tears left.

JUDITH KAZANTZIS

Eurydice

Eurydice never died.
It was Orpheus who went down
eagerly to the city of Hades.
He walked like a bandsman
with a broad back and the slung lyre
that had charmed all living things.

Birds, animals and Eurydice
followed the singer, whimpering and pleading
– She held up her arms
glowing in sun
but his back was turned on her;
he lost himself in the cloak flaps
of sumptuous Persephone, who
patrols the buried walls.
The mouth of the beast Cerberus
fed him down.

A venom bit
Orpheus, (maybe some snaky envy
of his own tongue?)
At any rate he died, and
the birds, beasts and weeping woman
climbed in a sad file
back through stalactites and rock lumps
to the small high-up sun.

Eurydice hoped to die, to
join him; but instead
seeing her white face
which was grief, not death,

I was sorry for her, and
I whispered, go to the shore.

I followed her discreetly
as her tears sprang down
on the brown and scarlet leaves.
We trudged through
a great planetree forest
to the sea. She took
the seashell, broken and chipped
but still iridescent
and zigzagged with amber words
as I'd set it for her;
it lay by the wave.

And that way, pressing
my shell to her ear, bending
to hear against the breaking
roar, as I'd suggested,
she heard her singer.
The dolphin and the seagull
flew from element to element
while Eurydice heard
his voice, Orpheus murmuring
marvellously from under the shore.

Under the slamming of the waves,
the young man's voice murmuring
to her: I am here, here
my love, in a glittering town.
I stand up in a tower
I see all Hades –
With my lyre
I call out the illustrious beauties
of this place, the beat
and hustle of its fires, the jewel
in the small flame, sea blue
or sea green, Eurydice my love.

She cries
into the zigzagged shell:
Orpheus come back – you're
wrong, you're in hell,
Orpheus my love, come back.
But the shell gives out one song
whispering, ecstatic.
Each minute a wave
roars, to block it.
Eurydice walks home
through scarlet leaves and the
cracked stumps of trees.

The shell
sits by the tidemark.
I followed her ten times to
that amber whorl and ten times
her expressive eyes
said, as she bent: my love,
my agony.
I was myself
hopeless and wiser. I hurled
the shell out to sea, on
an autumn tide: for the
fish to crowd in and
catch the blind corpse's
voice sing of fire:
and gawp and gape
in their pure shoals,
nosing for the singer.

SYLVIA PASKIN

Phases

white moon, new moon
blood runs to water
and staunches it

red moon, full moon
blood runs to fire
and changes it

black moon, old moon
blood runs to earth
and buries it

blue moon, the mystery where
blood runs to air
and touches it.

BERTA FREISTADT

Saffron's tree

I have a tree to show you
She said, she
Whose life story
Full of dying and rebirth
Had sat me still.

A tree in a field
Hiding its labours
Behind a perfect wall.
Tree growing from rock
Who grows with split bark
And bulging canker,
Cracking the grey rock ponderous
With whom nobody
Argues.

Ash, compliant wood,
Most easy cut,
Burns green.

That first naïve sapling
Sheltering in the nest
Made by protecting rock,
Hidden from the axe

Tendered from the snows,
That first sprout fresh,
So edible, observed by birds.
Overgrown plant not ready
For their resting claws.

How changed, how grown, outgrown
That rocky nursery.
Altered by frosts
And season's sneer.
Those branches bend
Down and often upwards.
Trunk span and stride,
With old arthritic gaiety now
Playing still and singing
With the wind.

See that tree
Whose body splits rock,
Root body and dancing twig.
Moves stone, the immovable past,
How did they lift them
Those lodestones?
How to move that immovable force
That flat resistance?
Only with the growing,
The running stream,
The accommodating bark
Which winds around
Thick,
And strong.
Drawing stone, penetrating
Cracks with
Its living finger.
Ash, vital wood,
Burns fast,
Cuts stone.

Tree out of rock,
Strong line.

Tree with your female
Crack
Held high out of reach
Of the dead rock.

Woman cracks slowly
With the pickaxe of will,
With wetness of love.
Exposed on those
Rocky places freezes,
Frozen expands
In the sought, hidden runnels
And there cracks angry
Pushing cold flint aside.

Ash alpha,
Ash alpha,
Burning, birthing twig.

We admired you.

JACKIE KAY

She kept her eye on winter

This woman thought in seasons
dreaming in autumn of making
the sunrise yellow leaves
into burnt orange wreaths
to comfort her dead with some colour
retaining those bright thoughts
before time withered
before the smile cracked into a plea
that remembered
times when their hands held
sorrows together when
midnight talks took
hold of the future.

How could those colours change that daring?

She dreamt that autumn of a summer
without falls as she tossed the morning
out of her nightmare as
she clung to each fall being
a bad dream; she kept her eye on winter
waiting for the snow to fall.

Remembering a time when
spring made the branches
blossom into soft surprises,
she closed her eyes as
the summer's heat shimmered
her black skin
tapping out new possibilities
– How can the summer be the same again
seasoned with this loss?
She forgot the pleasure of petals opening
when this young woman lay stiff
black dreams skeletoned
under the ground.

She knew the winter would come
again – bitter, bleak and blowing
its wide mouth extinguishing
each fragile dream of survival;
how to live on after this
when the face of night
meets the faces in the day
how to live on after this?

MICHÈLE ROBERTS

On Highbury Hill

that girl
with her sharp
hips, pelvic

bones jointed like sycamore
leaves that jerk and rock
down, she
with her boy's crop, hair
cut short as stubble in the corn
fields where fire and smoke
begin, scarlet heaps of burning
that collapse softly to black ash

she unexpectedly
came running out
of darkness, past
the iron spears of railings
the rattle of shadows guarding the park

I suddenly remembered her: she
whom I lost, who was hidden from me
for years in mists like this one: a
shiver of silver along the street, september
night arriving cold and solid as a gun

after a decade of absence

frost on the pavement
edge, evening air a chilly second
skin, my mouth
open, the wind in my throat
desire quickening me

VALERIE BLOOM

Interview

Oh, Miss Bloomfield – what? Oh, BROOMfield!
Sorry bout dat, come een, siddung,
Meck yuhsef comfortable, meck ah see now
Right, see di file yah – wait ah soon come.

Now where we wus? – Oh John, hold on
Yuh have a minute? How di wife?

Ah want to ax yuh bout di insurance policy
Yuh teck out wid Mutual Life.

Oh yuh busy, well gi mi a ring noh,
Yes man, call mi any time.
– Right, where we wus? – Oh John, John!
Di man coming Thursday fi di lime.

– Sorry bout dat mi dear Mrs Bloomfield,
Wha dat yuh sey? MISS BROOMFIELD, oh.
Bloomfield, Broomfield, noh matter really.
A meck dah phone haffe ring now doah?

Hello? hello? Oh Joe, a yuh!
Yes man, wha happen, den ow tings?
Mi mine dis run pon yuh yuh know
Yuh get di ting mi sen yuh? No man, no strings.

Den ow – Wha dat? Yuh lie! since when?
But dat no soun right! Fi wi Benny Green?
Den yuh mean to say from di time dem married
She noh know yet sey im nuffe eat soy bean?

No man, yuh naw interrupt nutten,
Galang chat, tell mi bout Flo.
Don' feget fi tell har yuh know,
Sey she must check mi out before she go.

Aright, see yuh, no man, babye –
Sorry bout dat, mi bredda yuh know,
From wi lef yahd dis mawnin mi noh see im.
But a whe mi ben a ax yuh now?

Oh yes, yuh benna sey – hole awn,
Peggy, quick, befo' mi fegat,
Yuh know dat letta mi beg yuh fi type.
Tell dem is a good ting wi noh employ Pigott.

Put i een mi sey or else
Mi wi put i een misef
Dem tink mi joke – Now Mrs Bloomfield,
– Oh, Peggy, send a copy to Mike an Jeff.

Now back to what wi wus saying Mrs B.
Wait a minute – Peggy, noh badda yaw,
Well cross i out, noh badda wid i,
Mi no able Jeff come bruck mi jaw.

But wait! A how time fly soh?
Twelve already? A when i get soh late?
Miss B. seems like yuh haffe come back tomorrow
Mi cyan tap now, mi hab a lunch date.

Oh, yuh live out in di country!
Well ah tell yuh what yuh do,
Lef yuh name an address wid wi
An wi will get in touch wid yuh.

See piece o paper yah, oh good
Yuh hab a pen aready.
Tank yuh Mrs Bloomfield, goodbye,
Hingh, Peggy, do supmn wi i.

CHERYL MOSKOWITZ

See me

See me, see me
(see right bloody through me)
I am not, no surely not
hiding nothing from you

So, Mr Psychiatrist – sit easy in your easy chair
and give me your prognosis
am I right in the head?

The latest survey I have read says
yes, you can lie in bed
and no one will know
they will even thank you, highly rank you
in the end
it is the trend
and only time, yes only time will mend.

So read me, read me
take your reports away and heed me
I will write you
yes, document you
in the end.

See me, see me
(see right bloody through me)

I'm on parade
a masquerade
for a position I don't want
I am expostulating frantic
sycophantic
to win your praise
your gaze
your evaluating stare
How do I fare?
Do I pass the what-you-want-me-to-be (you don't even care)
    examination?
I'm your creation
on display
this is the way
they always wanted it to be
see me, see me
(see right bloody through me)
My women friends, the girls
in coffee swirls
are so impressed
the loose bohemian way I dress
They are envying me my freedom
my freedom to choose
and so
would never think to accuse
the blank façade
it's even odd
that they will thank you, highly rank you (wind you up and crank
    you)
in the end.

BERTA FREISTADT

From the Semoi: dream modifiers

The Semoi are a people in Malaysia who train their children to control their dreams
for health, happiness, creativity and a sense of positive self.

I will not think of death
Anymore.
I will not let those dreams
Control my days.
I will be
Mistress of my night,
My own dream maker.

I will cast off
Those bondages.
The smell of burning
Rubber will offend your nostrils
As unwanted warpings
Ignite in the heat
Of my angry skin.

I will grow labia
Enormous as sunflowers
On my head to offend.
Some rogue growths
Developing thorns
And vengeful wills
Of their own,
I will not restrain.

When thrown onto burning pyres
My sisters and I will
Ascend immediately
To paradise
To celebrate their
Glorious and well-earned
Widowhood.

And those feet will
Learn to dance

Once more,
Sharp as needles
Trampling to compost
The weeping
Lotus petals.

When I dream of evil
In the future,
I will count your holes
And orifices
And tender innocent places,
(Feet, loins, forehead)
And manufacture
Hot ointment with them in mind.
Write texts books, fill libraries
With the tortured imaginings
I've learnt from you.
So fear and horror
Can be your companions
Too.

GRACE NICHOLS

My black triangle

My black triangle
sandwiched
between the geography
of my thighs

is a bermuda
of tiny atoms
forever seizing
and releasing
the world

My black triangle
is so rich

that it flows over
onto the dry crotch
of the world

My black triangle
is black light
sitting on the threshold
of the world

overlooking my deep-pink
probabilities

and though
it spares a thought
for history
my black triangle
has spread beyond history
beyond the dry fears of parch-ri-archy

spreading and growing
trusting and flowing
my black triangle
carries the seal of approval
of my deepest self

DEBORAH LEVY

Philosophers

You found her again, Honey Man
Extracting bee stings
In her sooty parlour

She was there to be found.

Your eyes, Long Lidded
and Lateral
Settle on her soul

Like the blue Inquisition:

She cracks sunflower seeds
Her bright eye laying
eggs in your ear

And you, scared of life
Curse woman for interfering.

She points to the map
With her sting. Listen
Honey Man. I am a salty
woman – been a long time
At sea. The Red Sea, The
Black Sea and sometimes
The Dead Sea. Unspeakable
Coral tearing at all I know.

I've come through.

He strokes his honeyduct
Tenderly. I've got a gift
For you. Want to give you
My libido for keeps. Want
to give you the stars –
Will starry words do instead?

I'll decorate you with my effort.

Honey Man, just give me
Your musk. I bang your words
Like tuning forks; they howl
Back like wolves. That is to say . . .
We might be soul mates

But never Comrades.

And their tears fell like tin
On poor dialectical roof tops.

STEF PIXNER

Whose fault?

1
Then, you were the freckled saint
who sighed and froze

and I the sinner, always

2
Outside, the claws of winter grip
the tree of heaven

a blizzard blinds the window
whipping quiet and white.

Inside, the tea is cold before it's poured
newspapers heap in deep drifts

like those in the road.
Cats scatter the landscape

of paper hills.

3
My memory plays like your cats
in the chaos

I remember days when the soup sloped south
and north where the warped table dipped

when your worn warm lap
was haven; kisses noon and night

rabbit turds and Arthur's knights together
on a bald baked lawn.

But then your red unruly hair
fierce halo

burned with blame.

4
Later I burned you too
I belched fire

for years I raked
charred bones.

You said I tried to kill you
I said you left me dead

you wronged me:
admit it! Admit it!

5
A fault is a deep crack
a single seam splits and slips

awry, and the two sides subside
forever separate

whose fault
is it?

6
Your light eyes startle
blue as before

tho' your long ago carrots
have turned to snow

7
The stove slowly warms the room

I take my coat off
sit back in my chair

look at the books
you've bought since I was here

you talk to me
of Moscow's boozers

and of Albania's ancient kings

8
And you laugh now
under the bare bulb

wavering over the depths,
no blame

it's with others
that now I burn and burn.

V

THE IN-TIDE

MARK WILLIAMS

Descriptive poem

Your hair is on fire,
And George Eliot has started a new paragraph.
I cannot help you,
I cannot move,
Until the paragraph is over.
We are walking through sentences.
We are picking wild flowers.
Your hair is a landscape,
It is beautifully described.
George Eliot looks up from her writing.
'There is a smell of burning in the air',
She says to me.
Your hair is on fire,
Yes, your hair is on fire
And George Eliot has started a new paragraph.
I cannot help you,
I cannot move,
Until the paragraph is over.
We are walking through sentences.
We are picking wild flowers.
Your hair is the colour of the sky.
It is beautifully written.
George Eliot looks up from her writing.
'This is not description, I fear',
She says to me.
Your hair is on fire
And George Eliot has started a new paragraph.

MARY MICHAELS

The ice land

In memory of John, 1944–1975

I walked to the middle of the world last night
it might have been called *Ice-land* or *Green-land*
– a high plateau with prairie grass –
but it wasn't in the north and there was no ice

Huge clouds were gathering speed
from the edge of a miles away horizon
each rolling forward singly, swiftly
against an unvarying hard blue sky
and the air was so absolutely clear
you could see the shape of the rock everywhere

Inside a wooden house – very clean –
my brother lay looking out of the window
the room was illuminated and white
with light from the landscape although it was evening
the place was beyond sun setting, sun rising

I was about to say goodbye
then I realised the room was lonely
the house and the whole vast country were empty
with only the clouds that rolled inwards moving
he was alone – entirely alone – in the ice land

and I had to leave him

STEF PIXNER

Near death

Near death
she halts

bent, brown, ninety
smelling rank.

She's peeled
the family photos

from the walls
leaving pale patches

bare of dust
like the rubbed out patches

of her memory.

'Is it Saturday today?
day or night, is it?'

At last she's happy
the bitterness of unlived passions

rubbed out too.

Cunningly young
she smiles, bends

fiddles a red rose through my button hole.
'My darling girl!'

Its sharp stalk
tickles the skin

between my breasts.

BARBARA BURFORD

Dying

Dying gets easier.
There is almost
no other choice.
The true lover,
asking nothing,
but me.

No more rejections,
no more bloody

bruised hands,
held out.
See – I love you.

Just the deep
dark violet cruise,
out of this
out of here
into bliss.
Into nothing.
My own space.
At last.

PASCALE PETIT

The sea at dawn

A hopeless dawn
And the sea is high
Mother – you couldn't
Comfort me – the tide
Was always out. I cried
For days and nights
But not enough, the sea
Alone would hold
The salt in me.

You lay there
Beyond grasp
I who was born too soon,
You in your pack of ice
Rot in your womb.

I needed your love
Then, as I do now
But you had glass arms
And your tears were frost
On my case-glass.

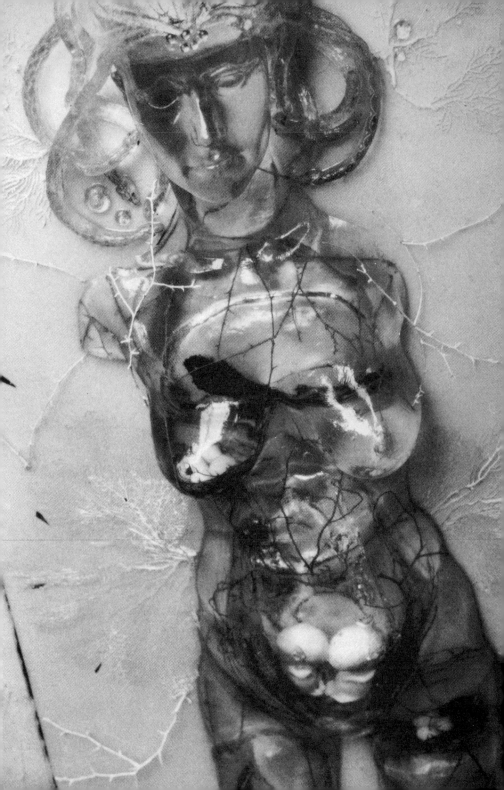

Your drawn face is etched
On the living-room pane
And I am not born yet.
The sea is high
Your tears float there
And mix with mine.

But you are locked
In a translucent zone
And it is long ago
Since we were one.
They must have implanted
Me in you, I suppose,
For no man
Could have clasped
You in their arms
Woman of snow.

I look through the window
And I am no-one
Just sperm and foam.
You always wanted
Me to go
Back through the glass
Into your vulva
Your alien soul
And fling me, fling me
Back to the dark

But you can't mother
You were not able
The tide was always too cold, too far,
Forget all your tears
I don't need you mother –
– My darker face
In the old mirror,
I have another one
Whom I call day
You disappear with her

SARA BOYES

Kite

The wind is very weak today he says. But I say
I see kites flying high. She

has eyes this kite. She has a head and
her eyes are demure. Closed. But her tails

betray that simpering sweetness. Her tails
legs, strips of red glistening

cellophane the sun glints on shines
through, flip and flit and run in trembles

pulled out on the string she yearns
on the tips of her many toes. Her toes tip

and eagerly tremble and patter
on the air, and wave and flicker and

stream out in red flickering waves, eager
pulling to be off. I say I see kites flying

high. He says the wind is very weak today. In-
expert his hand pulls to find

the place for her where she'll sail free. But she
drops. This body swimming to keep head above in the

air. Running on the spot near the ground, wiggling
cellophane streamers flapping. Head

turning this way that to
regain the freedom up high there. The wind

is very weak today he says. But
I say I see kites flying high.

NICKI JACKOWSKA

Opening the river

Today I am woman coming to the edge of water
to wash linen caked with dust. How air resists
my thighs, pushing through. How water clasps me
blue at the foot, white froth on my raking hand.

I haven't been here before, this bowl of water.
The trees are talking thin today. I don't know
how the rinsing water is dissolving threads
my legs are water-quiet, pitched against flood.

Lifting like sacrifice, the basket creaks wide with sun
its clothes stiffened with earth, their spines crack.
Water sparking out of clay, my shoulder is a bending
hollow; when I enter, river holds there smiling.

JANET SUTHERLAND

To Patricia (Paddy)

in all this is the courage
you will not sing
mouthing the words at weddings and funerals
in dim churches

once with the sound of the tractor
in the fields you opened your mouth
and let rip
till you knew the low drone of the engine
still let the song out into the open field

with what courage you stumble and fall
work in the cowsheds   dip cold hands in hot water
milk knit garden   moving around the house
in a dance with the sound of the song pouring
around and inside you stopping just short of your mouth
in your mind you sing defiantly
making light
of your body

PENELOPE TOFF

From the Eype's mouth

Become like children
     amidst the sprawling
Grey fingers of clay
Where the source has seeped
       and dribbled onto sand
Sadness is there when
Emerging
   from running underground
The Eype pours out relentlessly
Echoing of diminutive beginnings
The in-tide beats stones
Into something more precious
  And stacks them
  Against cliffs
We exposed fear pieces
      which break away
Forgetting
   how the whole has come to be

WENDY MULFORD

'How do you live?'
For Hélène Cixous, who gave me the question.

no clear answer, ambivalently.
reciprocally.   in
oscillation.   lurching in surprise &
wonder. an
after-effect of too much pricy
delegation, herein described as
daringly/close to
disaster, danger's cousin. I sd you can
drop a mile or two before the bank-rate rises then lie back my sweet

& take it,   a curt remedy
after too much attempted,
a hot needle to the index tip, tags
of clipped hair shed from the nape
in instant dispersal the broken sump
evenly coating the labour we
unevenly perform – oh there is
too much talk & what is shared in timid
in timid recoil does not nor ever can
satisfy the heart, these ultra-private
accommodations between person &
politics negotiating survival while
the sea rises hold on for what you can
I sd, or
'a woman's place behind the home
everywhere & nowhere fear
of placeness, hold on
for what we can, cradling
cuddling care. home love
tucked body refuge will satisfy what part?'

1979

DINAH LIVINGSTONE

Nerve

Roof leaks, stop it with sticky tar,
thick and black like a babe's first shit.
Wall cracks, we imperfectly plaster it
with a slapped mixture of pinkish powder.
Light bulbs break, we are in the dark,
drains block and the sludge reeks of decay.
Propping and prodding keep the frail pad cosy
and fickly hold the primal soup in check.

Neither can we ban weakness from this bonehouse;
I bleed, I ache, I alter every day.
Skull lurks, disintegration stalks us,

I am unwomaned when I've had no tea.
I only find my centre now and then,
when good animal spirits give a shove
or where beyond tiredness joy slips in:
ocean, eros, here-earthly union, love.

And when I spin in centrifugal panic,
feel dizzy as the velvet night wears thin,
I do not flee the hound of heaven frantic
but from the hole I fear is where my centre should have been.
String snaps, I collapse, am disassembled.
How now scrap antiquated parts; add; see
whether this heap of heterogeneous junk all jumbled
fits back together another way?

Constantly. This is the price of every poem
and of living, every time it snarls up, wisdom.
The permanent point is cordial
being both membership and individual.
It needs a great heart not to deviate into religion,
courage to utter, endure chaos, utter anew,
nerve not to give up making and, with knots between,
thread blood-red garnets, despite what death will do.

LIBBY HOUSTON

Childe Roland takes on the dark tower one more time

– Sheer tower in the wood, black hole in the hill,
   dark doorway with a grand canyon cracking the sill,
   seen it once a hundred times, where the stick of ragwort
   stakes out its little world take off your hat to it –

   *Childe Roland, a woman this time round, looks up
   from the maps on her lap, her faithful squire's the driver:*

– This is the place, this is it, now or never – again.
Like the man said, some Viking in a tight saga,
One's back is bare without a brother, brother,
so keep me covered, I'm going in alone

– Hey wait a minute –
you forgotten what day? The time?
The kids? The tickets? Your mother? Look – I booked the room!
You tell me nothing, you, your shabby shoes, what's the
score? What's in that rats' Ritz
any concern of yours?

– I don't know, not yet –
ghoul guardian gunman friend fiend – me or it:
shifting in black, I know that, smell or touch
tells enough in the quiet quiet; but it decides
the weapons, picks the game

So when my back's turned on you now turn yours –
stare, and you'll fix me, throw me bare
like arclights on the wire – don't shoot me down!

I need someone you here keeping this coast clear
and the engine ticking over, the kids fed – just act
for these clothes of mine, be my disguise, if I'm not back
I will be –

> *Out now, kerbside, she's*
> *ten-ton grey against black gloss,*
> *bending and turned to*
> *his shade-barred gaze not far off*
> *belt-level – he's too*
> *armchair, too well-placed:*

– You drag me all this way pour
crap in my ear? Guess you better
run off and play then. Dear. I'll give you
half an hour. While I adjust my set. I get!
I'll count, what is it? eighteen hundred? starting
NOW! And that's it. One –

– Oh you make easy reading, ask you to walk a mile and you'll
head two, the other direction, fast – why not tie my hands
behind my back if you like? Go on, hook the day on tight
and when you're hungry, reel it in, reel it in, you'll find
your dead umbrella on the line again –
so eat it

– OK you too hero, one of these pleading
whales hooked on doom, tell you life's
fun makes you growl – well, it's up to you what you choose,
cross that step, don't, don't look for me again

I'll write you from Athens.
If I think of your name –

> *Fade-out, the dust goes with him;*
> *the spidereyed brickwork settles to ringside seats,*
> *spotlights tacked to her feet:*

– Black doorway dribbling wet trash through its
gums, my lucky dip, same river twice
a hundred times, and every time
one foot gets stuck in the bank

Stumbling up like the fool I know I look
to be beaten at half-cock on the brink again, I think
much more of this, and I ought to come out hammered tough as
the Iron Man. Wrought. Proof. No, me more likely
flat as a boneless wonder from a Norse bog

The thing is,
what's there's been the one so far with time at its
side, handing the scalpel, wiping the brow
and sending out this call sign I seem rigged to read
Drop what you're doing, it's now –
when it fancies, or when it remembers, or
I just happen to cross its moving waveband

So – how if I just strolled by
your doors, your panting mouths,
maybe chuck in a stone, and say

'You can wait. I'll come in when it
suits me'?

By that I mean armour. Or
nakedness – now that
could cancel the bad step!
What am I going for the front?
Next time I start dead centre,
uncovered, the thing itself.

ALLEN FISHER

From: Banda

Took chances in London traffic
where the culture breaks
tone colours burn from exhaustion
emphasised by wind,
looking ahead for sudden tail lights
a vehicle changes
lanes into your path and birds,
over the rail bridge, seem purple.
A mathematician at the turn of the century
works out invariant notions in a garden
every so often climbs a bike,
makes a figure of eight around
rose beds to help concentration,
then returns to the blackboard.
The schemers dreamed a finite language
where innocence became post-experiential
believing the measurable, ultra-violet from a lamp,
isolated sunlight curvature
made false language what can be done
to separate
from perception.
In a dream apparently without volition
a car burning and
watch myself there

sealed-in beneath a smog dome
uncertain what to try for next.

Midnight: a solo of the Nightingale. Great silence.
Open a gate
against hinged pressure of rust,
white pigment to denote reflected light.
Singularity burgled up the drain pipe,
a busy rush pursued tenderness at its slats
padlocked into pastoral quicksilver.
'If one of my students should one day rear children
in a better way'
Surround myself in music, that is physically
forget the dream as a move towards preventing
objectification of vision.
Legal power, completion, smothering,
on the shelf flashpowder and a can.
Practice to assist improvisation
holds onto the pattern of railings
a superstructure of sound-curve symmetry
recognised, and examined, by autodidacts.
A bunch of type in my palm
populates fixed compartments.

Exasperation from a lack of clarity
sighs towards singular objectives
trapped into them
without realising
the peripheral fleets
glanced at knowingly
as an indefinite refusal
of euphony,
or until the variety gets coded
into an analytic container
dropped from a winch onto the quay.
When the road shifted
one part lowered
then pushed out a halting arm
over the ridge

carrying a reflex camera
to record the wonderful.
A recollection of a hill so far from London
I burnt lying
in a dream for thirty minutes
and woke in a grove of oranges
smelling of eucalyptus.
The up and down different to anyone
gravity
or opposes anthropologists of science.
It took six minutes for the exercise
and the lot was cordonned off,
Water Lane
to Brixton Oval,
our future in the air
over the walkway busted polystyrene
scattered,
a sonata for piano and jetplane,
cooperatively struct,
now a mount of cars piled behind a subsiding dyke.

4 a.m. the Hedge Sparrow, shriek of the Hoopoe,
the Song Thrush on trumpet,
a large ball rolls by
hits the sentry box
and the road opens.
On one side a ley line buckles
into the wall of 'The George',
in the machine a solenoid blows
a rush of green vans and police weapons
send the needles into peak
and damage the Dolby.
Your freckles expand and you blush,
a black clock and two batteries,
my fingers tingle to let the blood back
we roll over
temporal inversions or points of view
burn the air,

and memory, slatted into alternations,
begins to rely on the instrument panel
as well as the force
felt in the chest
as speaker loudness increases.
The explanation of the universe gets
considered as shared awareness and truth
a bucket with a hole in it slops suds over
the top onto a tiled floor
until we switch it off.

Two electricity lines,
three gas mains,
carry enough energy across the walkway
for two sets of loudspeakers
face each other across the
dancing
visitors at an island of science
see the primitives at work
describe the utility of pilot lights.
The furniture in the room appears to be stationary.
I am half sick of shadows
under pressure of personal feelings
a poet crushes a carton marked 'Shredded Wheat'
in a corn field,
calls it a poem.
Laid out on the lawn
exhausted
the burden of personality lost
in untimed contemplation
independent of unified law
uses signs for other
than what they signify
by filling navel with powder
and exhaling a cough.
I suppose it is in me and coming out.
The quantum leap
between some lines
so wide
it hurts.

MARY MICHAELS

Dream and Five Interpretations

The ceiling was covered with caustic spray
in danger of burning
  it *had* been burning
the surfaces of the walls and floor
were peeling and searing
flaking and fuming
a bubbling jet of corrosive acid
down by the fireplace
wouldn't turn off
the room that was meant to have been
the bedroom
  the main room
was ruined
and dangerous

I am the room in danger of burning
fuming and farting
flaking and peeling
my skin is the ceiling
my hands the floor
  dry and scoured and scorched
  and sore
I'm charred with a scarring
that won't heal up

I am the acid bubbling and running
  viscous
  combustible
  overflowing
out of this fuel
the flame shot over
I am the fear of it
I am the flame

I am the child who discovers the fire
  priggish
  purposeful
  'Little Red Riding Hood'
grasping the jet
I can't get it turning
  the foam may be harmful
  the foam may be good

MARK WILLIAMS

Smoky throat

My legs won't work
Got a smoky throat
Voice keeps telling me
About a blue sky boat

Breeze in my chest
Blows down a tincan
Can you read my mind?
What am I thinking?

If I dropped down dead
What would you do?
There's only three feet of ground
Left – to dig into.

I'm in the middle of the road
Traffic all around me
Watch me dance!
The road is the sky.
Watch me dance!
I can't fall down.

All aboard the blue sky boat
Paradise is here
Heaven's all around us
You don't have to be

A spiritual recluse
You don't have to be
Highly educated
There's no need to cut your throat
Just climb aboard
The blue sky boat

I got one bad leg
I got two good eyes
That's two good legs
And one bad eye

Take a walk in the forest
Take a stroll in the sun
See the dragonflies flying
You're back where you begun.

Take your places, please
This is no time for thought
Let's be on our way
On board the blue sky boat.

Where are we going?
We're off into space.
Going nowhere.
Going to that place.

GRAHAM HARTILL

Ghost Dance

the Earth is yellow
the Earth is blue
listen to this rhyme
grandfather
in your scorching nail factory, 1924
listen to my song
grandmother
stringing up rabbit-meat in your grocery shop
doing your accounts

the Earth is brown & wet
there is rain pouring on gaslit streets
take account of this song grandmother
it is pouring with rain

the Earth is white
the Earth is red
the bird may be dead
but the feather is still flying
the whirlwind blew
& your faces became water
the sun shines on that running water
I can hear you
walking between the stars
I can hear you
patrolling up & down through time
this is
      the Ghost Dance

the snow lies here & there
& the Earth turns –
we walk out onto the promontory
St David's Head
full of soft green stones
the sea dusted with light
& the stream fizzing
this is
      the Ghost Dance
there is a fire in the plain
& there is no song to be heard in the hills
but that of the wind only
this is
      the Ghost Dance

– the wild stars.
I see a good many faces before me.
My own parents' faces – my father's
ageing over the years, friendly & strong
& tired, working in the car-factory

for over 20 years, two weeks on day-shift,
two weeks on night-shift. He asks me
if I've got any money in my pocket –
I show him a couple of fivers & he says
'you're okay then?' Bear father
out hunting every day, watching
over his brood, looking after their stomachs.
And my mother's face now, 72 & still going strong,
looking after her brothers & sisters
through the 30's & the War
when my grandfather was out of work,
her beautiful, dark & respectable
late 20's face in a photo
on the living-room wall.
And a bit later, straight after marriage
her war-time face.

*

at Patshull,
   a duck takes off from the lake,
      droplets
     drip from its feet
   arcing green neck,
     shining, skyward

      this is
         the Ghost Dance

with the wind
  caught in his strings
Mr V plays it

  & the tapes revolve

   transmit

    genetic geography.

   accelerating lacework
    of guitar & synthesizer

citrine lichens
spreading across the dead birch

*

the field is yellow
the field is red
listen to the snow
grandchildren
& to the heat.
the field is brown & wet
there is wind in the streets.

the sky is green
grandchildren
the sky is white.
I wonder where you live?
the ground reclaims
its own life.

this is
the Ghost Dance
this is   the breadword
the grassword the colourword
this is
the message of the genes
this is
my tongue my eyes my testicles

the city is our fathers
the city is
our mothers
the city is our grandfathers
grandmothers
daughters, our sons

or our faces be turned to the wall

the city of wind
the city of travellers

the city of day
the city of grass

JUDITH KAZANTZIS

Swinging

Sonny Rollins
stood on Brooklyn Bridge
for four years
and blew and blew   figuring
this and that
after Bird died   and
                              until
he was clear to walk forward again.

They say you could hear the sax
groaning and crying
above the percussions of the cars
and the barely pounding bass
    wind over the East River
       all day fisting
    across one thousand cables

Like a feather
          brushing sunlight
                On its own   until

it came for earth again

flew like silver in a cool fever
                    into Manhattan.

SUE MAY

To the Angel

She takes me for a ride to the black of night
it's all right, I want to go there
She helps me
We are friends.

The car belonged to a hitman
She rubbed him out on St Valentine's Day
She tough
Her ices are like eyes.

Now she is warm
I loll in the car seat
The street-lights come towards us
And go over our heads.

The car is a zip in the blackness
She talking but not with words
I hear the sounds
She gargles with Tequila Sunrise

In the dark
I can see the rocks in her eyes
Once they were snow
and would melt

Sometimes they are diamonds
not now though
now she is warm
and my face is wet.

THE SYNTAX OF VISION

LOTTE MOOS

Joy

Here's no tiger riding the city
In a chariot of teeth, streets blazing percussion
Just a small creature pointing a small blunt snout
Round the half-open door
And no one mentioned 'Come in'

Here's no crashing of fire engines banging big bells
'Help! Let me quench this fiery passion'
Only a tangled look, given and taken
For keeps (finders are keepers)
To fill the sluice of the heart
And it leaps

Or a word, an image, jumps like a fish and whirls round the finger
Clarity opens its fan, definition unfurls between pencil and nose
And we smile: 'This is how it is'
– Darkness recedes

Think, how many spindles of joy
Can dance on the point of a needle
Against grim gravity's pull
– How many, O Lord, how few?

So, let's issue a proclamation
An order of preservation for you but also for me
We herewith declare, stake
The inalienable right
Of mice in the trap
To the last-ever delight
Of imponderables, token caresses, mere sleight-of-hearts
Windows hanging, on half-broken sashes, into the world
Trial balloons afloat, curled like pompoms, a second or two
Before they go Pfhh
In the air, go Pfhh
And the ashes come down

GEOFFREY GODBERT

The world has yet to be named

The world has yet
to be named
from the deep silence
of a womb.

The world has yet
to be named,
it is within, searching
like a foetus.

The world has yet
to be named
from its perfect
concealment.

The world has yet
to be named;
dark rhythms form an ear,
eyes seek out their colour.

The world has yet
to be named,
aching like birth
for release.

The world has yet
to be named,
a cry will begin
its identity.

The world is about
to be named
the unendurable word
out of love.

JAY RAMSAY

To The Swan
For S.

1

Something gives, swan comes up ashore, I write
The word awe in the middle of a white page –
A window of tense space fading like mist,
Leaving this morning sun that blurs and then cleanses
Eyes that turn out content to be watching
Curtains thrown back to the sea, moving . . .
To headland and horizon – a line spread
Out of buzzing wakefulness: swan tipping her bill back,
To catch each last bright shaking of falling drops;
Drawing this raw world into the shape of her slow glide.

The open door shows a path and a leading on,
Stronger than a thin thread of doubt that hesitates.
I am opening this same door once more – again:
To take this journey that is being thought through me.

This is the path, and it goes to the sea.
And this is the sea and the sound that is healing me.

2

Wind on cliff – wild around you;
Blown yellow gorse flowers – tossed hair –
Impossible to talk, walking, breathing in, lungfuls
Dive-eyes down into the sight of those amazing pounding waves.
Sound of air and water as a mirror
Of lightened storm sky, puffed blue,
And a cow behind us pissing squat-legged on dung earth.
This is the place, and we are connected
By spirit of skin-fire, voice
That utters us, as human, as near
And as far away

As a small white sail.

Walk on searching the waving ploughed ground;

Comb a useless piece of china bowl, and cherish a stone
Of fossilised, remembered earth

And tiny luminous needles of new corn.

Nothing of either time or date
Only chimes that echo ... this pause
And evaporate, back to the yackering
Distracted ravens shading in through big cedars.
The dead are all here in the long shadows,
And we are given over here; the place is Roseland,
And there is no more God than this wild garden

Where a robin comes as close as two hands.

3
Night signals that whisper on the air,
We are the signal here

Touch down softly bent down over our knees
With the tide coming in and each reach of wave
Runs out and drains, quick-quick-slow caressing
Of shingle kiss and tongue tip delved to soundless
Mouthing it body rapt bliss of us brings us to shimmering;
Silvered as stranded fish dreamily gasping for air –
Swim into a long lingering spiral let loose
Ah with that love, at length, at last, which breaks
Down our selves

Into this sky-sized open eye.

And the calm is a sea
Of flung back sheets.

And the calm
Is inviolate.

4
Reaching the other side, reaching an island
Breast-stroke for miles under moonlight;
And the man is seated in a chair, bowed down,
Shivering at the ritual of his secret fears

Then he goes to the water's edge
Bare feet on sand; waits, and then wades in
Up to his waist, waits, and then falls in
Floating out as if dead, and with no direction
You found him washed up all sodden and wooden,
You covered him up in his sleep of death
You let him dream his broken fevers
Till the grub inside of him began to grow
With wings sheathed for flight,

As you stand; with your arms outstretched
Guarding the only possible
One last vision.

5
And you take me over and you take me down,
Hardly knowing what I'm supposed to find
Wandering over the lush mound of green
Down, in a steep slope and the grass grows
Above my head, and the air is warm and humming,
As the path ends on a half-hidden beach –
An upturned boat, small slabs of grey stone

And this swan; waddling about, stretching her neck
Distended, beauty, preening her ruffled feathers, graced
Brought into what I am, and what I can't translate
There is only this crazy caring gesture to make
Against absolute nothingness: she comes out
And through this never-ending ending;

Wings raised up with a sudden croak
Up into their full flaring span,

And out of me, pouring into the sun-stream.

GILLIAN ALLNUTT

New Year Poem, 1984

I need a holiday in wood or bread
or stone, a hard
mediterranean

light, a big lump of it
and hands that can make it
mourn merrily.

I need a clean wind, hunger
choosing a land
of its own:

not a war
of words or wills or chicken wire
but battles in bone,

in blood. I need those who have died
believing in it, even if
it was stupid.

I need a man and a woman made of light,
between them
not a wooden god, but

one that doubts and ponders
until all that was made
ill is mended.

DINAH LIVINGSTONE

Peace

Lovely curve of hill
is a mild ox resting at noon.
There at last sit still.
Empty tins that clattered in my head,
a mountain of litter discarded,

rag and bone man makes a killing.
Now a mild ox at noon,
I listen to the gorse pods popping.

On the train the sweetbriar brat
is a wild skilled irritation
to the dove-soft mother
drained dry grey with exhaustion.
The continual din persists
that whole wilderness-long journey.

The receptionist copy typist,
neat and clean through an exact discipline,
expertly flicks switches,
trying to connect you, simultaneously
types the curious prose –
she is scrupulous – of their busy effusions,
or tabulates sterling noughts.
She has sore eyes, a sick headache,
pulse ticks, successfully
polite all day, goes home a wreck.

And the glistering party girl
on a mega-rave, spinning, spinning.
Those decibels definitely deafen,
mum warns take care.

And in cornflower sunlight of huge desire
autumn touches the park.
Lads wheel barrows, Shakespeare knew them.
Greasy merchants on the pickup
stalk disconsolately unattractive.
Friends sit and talk.
Near the fountain where late roses bloom
a couple who now have made
just over a century between them
kiss and stroll on.

And let peace come
like cornflower sunlight on September trees,

like sweetness into fruit,
grass smell, warmth to the earth.
Let peace come,
noise cease for a little while,
listen with inward ear
now to the cordial voice,
listen well with imagination
to friends and all those strangers.

Peace possess all.
Let it steal onto your lap
like a favourite cat,
over your face like a smile,
catch you and hearten unawares
like a cheerful tune with rhythm.

Let peace come
to the party-girl, the dove-soft mother
and the receptionist copy typist.
Listen to the gorse pods popping.

Be spared that other explosion.

FRANK BANGAY

Solidarity

I cried last night
But my tears were a mirror
Of the sadness in the world,
The earth throbbed loudly
A strong beating heart.

A tree cried last night
Its leaves drifting
Downwards in the laughing wind.
A tree bled last night
When someone cut its bark
And let its sap flow freely.

And we stood under the stars
Our fragile bodies
Swaying in the wind,
We counted the years
And shared experience.
We were cleansed of pain.

We cried together last night
But our tears were in solidarity
With the sadness in the world;
And through our solidarity
Through our tears, we found strength.

ALAN JACKSON

This is it

this ground this dream these myths
this time this place this river
we broken people, this ugliness, this empty,
not yonder, not elsewhere, not the fault of,
none of this caused by causes accessible
to ology, ism or hate;
there's been no mistake here, no wrong turning:
this is the sum of our fate
this is it
this is where we stand and make choice,
see what we've done and accept it as ours
must read the world till it comes transparent
and then be ready for Voice,
for loosening the grip of matter from our minds;
re-assertion of the Infinite
re-admission of the Divine
this is it
this hysteria this ignorance these cages,
these times this violence this darkness
they're what we believe and feel   written on the world
and when we sicken of looking at shadows

we can look for the light within
for there is light
but first we find what throws the shadows
– bitter reckoning, painful wrestling, guilt
quite startling, to minds unused to struggle,
consciences accustomed to blame
another

ah then the stories become realities,
then the myths grow wings and fly
then the creatures we tidied away
appear to sting and cackle and cry

ah then the mind begins to wander
then the mask begins to crack
then one tear that slips unasked for
's welcome like mercy to soul on the rack

for see how badly we've treated the earth
see how badly we've treated ourselves:
we have denied there was feeling in feeling things
we have denied there was life in living things
we have extinguished and mutilated species
we have analysed the adrenalin of frightened creatures;
wearing blinkers, we have said, 'I can't see it',
clad in iron, we have said, 'I can't feel it',
we have handled butterflies with tongs and said:
'This is nothing but fragments'
all to be reckoned, all to be paid for
by each living soul
so

if unsure, then good, for therefore attention
if loss, the good, for therefore find
if pain, then good, for therefore openings
if alone, then good, for therefore listen
if hardship, then good, for therefore strength
if poor, then good, for therefore simple
if death, then good, for therefore birth.

CHRIS TORRANCE

I see

I SEE	fluctuant red sand molecule
I SEE	the cranebird's
	word in the sky
I SEE	molten pressure of the heaving earth
I SEE	the heavy metal oceans
I SEE	the agglomerate of horizons
I SEE	nuke boats glowing on the seabed
I SEE	Aries rising
I SEE	the silver spear pierce the alimentary drum
I SEE	the ripple of
	continental shields folding
I SEE	tectonic grind in the basement disco
I SEE	shattered punks
	their teeth are like stars
I SEE	motorcycle fanbelt in the road
I SEE	infinity in a cracked mirror
I SEE	joy
	in a wrecked aero engine
I SEE	blue barrows in the orange grass
I SEE	porno flicks
	in Caesar's diary
I SEE	the paradox of nationhood of warring clans
I SEE	pyramid cement harder than the atom
I SEE	no space without life
I SEE	dharma sufferers, without requite
I SEE	mass media hype
I SEE	torn skylines of greed
I SEE	bearers of
	dogmatic hate & prejudice
I SEE	tigers of the deep with glowing eyes

I SEE   the demon
                        prowl the fault lines

I SEE   the riddle of the universe
I SEE   the chicken & the egg
I SEE   frogspawn eye of the Creator
I SEE   that fission is ecstasy

I SEE   the shanks of the mountain move
I SEE   the bricks of the ziggurat fall
I SEE   the Towers
                        of Transportation
I SEE   pearly haze of industrial beauty
I SEE   the miasma
                        of the people's discontent
I SEE   the Van Allen belt
                                with a pulsing hole in it
                                its unity suffers pain
I SEE   the planet undergoing
                                forced electrotherapy

I SEE   two trumpet shapes in a storm cloud
I SEE   three halves of the globe,
                        ego   bombast   & pestilence
I SEE   no devil exists
                        but the one inside
                        us . . .

I SEEEEEEEE EEEEEEEE EEEEEEE EEEEEE EEEEE EEEE
   EEE EE E

JEREMY SILVER

The Open

Eating wild strawberries
cherries out of season
not English but Russian
Hebrew voices fill me
with their beauty as I read

slow rich poetries
whose crimson words
suffer darkly
spread over the page
translations send me
juices of berries
spill around lips
blur the sources
of their flushed colour
fill me with hope
and acid the sweet
tang of hard expression
citrus jets that glisten off
under the shade of trees
in a far different forest
from where the flowers first grew

and in that uneasy transformation
of brambles into torn verbs
I listen to my sisters' voices sing
our mouths are ringed   stained
by the same strange fruits
which only grew in distant plantations
seem to spring into bloom from our veins.

JOHN AGARD

Go spread wings

If I be the rain
you be the earth
let love be the seed
and together
make we give birth
to a new longing
for harmony growing
among all things
and love go spread wings
love go spread wings

If I be a tree
clinging to parch earth
this time you be the rain
and love the wind
taking we by the hand
showing the way
to new awakenings
among all things
and love go spread wings
love go spread wings

TONY LOPEZ

Poem about swallows

Many times I have washed my hands
Now it seems I think only of skin.

The skin of lemons is shiny wonderful
But banana is always a routine.

I don't like to do the same thing
Some days I throw out all the socks

And start again: Bleach hurts,
And scouring powder, a cotton rag –

The little stain under the tap. I lost
The poem about swallows that mentions

'Delicate air' so there is an end of it.
But on a damp day, close to the ground –

Or floating on the surface of a pond,
I might remember just what it was.

SYLVIA PASKIN

Utsuroi

You will never locate beauty in space or time.
But only through yielding to the delicate fraud
Of any smile and accepting that when water ripples,
It has more innocence than a dream.

An urgent, leaping shadow at the heart of movement
Betrays the frozen constancy of things and reveals
Their divine evanescence. There is a vertigo to
All that trembles under the light.

And at this point of change, an interval of
Emptiness, a fugitive void, the soul flies –
Has already left and joyously has not yet
Met the other.

Utsuroi is a Japanese concept which depends on the understanding that time is not linear, not one event after another in a chain, but an overlapping sequence of the same shapes – as in a shaken kaleidoscope.

JANET SUTHERLAND

'Spent a day in talk'

Spent a day in talk
and a day turning the earth
two actions
one consequence

dream of that courtyard
pillars, the dry dust
on the road
sitting the whole day
placed

but how to achieve it here
hustled by small goals

in their anger
and mine
and partake?

i will not believe all this is
is endurance
there was joy in the recognition
and learning to care
is the other thing

turn to your friend and embrace her
pull the long roots of aggression
make a good soup from the nettle.

PAUL A. GREEN

From: The slow ceremony
For Cathy

What signal is being communicated by the rain? No fancy in the flux
of water, these molecules licking through the air,   their halo
over and all around, to liquidate the syntax of vision in visions – it's
all suggestive – 'Know what I mean'

In the rain the thing is. The thing is that flutter of water that
flattens the rank grass, out there, out front, like all pleasures in
the wet hedges it's a tiny incandescent thing. You know. All about
the rain.

We like the recurrence of rain, the soft pattern, its grey beat.
No shame in admitting a preference for tree dwelling, 'entirely
surrounded by water'. We're in. It's out.

But that isn't the whole signal. A reading of the rain goes (and grows)
well beyond that. The rain states that the swimming of small lights,
the drench of fallen stars, what we fabricate in darts and glances, all
that – and *you* know what I mean – is, simply, the right forest to
pick ferns in.

TONY LOPEZ

Hart's-tongue

See how leaves build at the fences
And years or trees equally
Come to be believed. No one will
Speak of this unless we speak –
How the green and yellow surfaces
Do silently gleam. Had we but
Come to ourselves in the forest
We should have heard a rustle –
Among the lady and ladder-ferns,
Leading to nowhere but a deeper green.

NOTES ON THE CONTRIBUTORS

John Agard was born in Guyana in 1949, came to England in 1977, and works as a Touring Lecturer for the Commonwealth Institute. He calls himself a 'poetsonian' because he feels a kinship with the satirical spirit of folksy calypso music. His publications include *Limbo Dancer in Dark Glasses* (1983). He was the winner of the Casa de las Americas poetry prize in 1982 for his cycle of poems about steel-pan music, *Man to Pan*.

Gillian Allnutt was born in 1949. She is the author of *Spitting The Pips Out* (Sheba, 1981) and has a collection of poems forthcoming from Virago. She is poetry editor at *City Limits* magazine and sometime member of the 'Angels of Fire' collective.

Frank Bangay was born in 1951. In the 70s he helped start various community poetry groups, gigged/recorded with musicians especially 'The Fighting Pigeons'; currently active member of British anti-psychiatry movement in CAPO (Campaign Against Psychiatric Oppression) – involvement borne of years of experience under psychiatry; believes poetry can offer hope to others, demystify mental health issues, clarify and heal, the personal and political being forever connected.

James Berry came to Britain in 1948, and has lived and worked here ever since. A full-time writer since 1977, his first two collections of poems were *Fractured Circles* and *Lucy's Letter and Loving*. He has performed his poetry in venues around the country and on BBC radio. He has edited an anthology of Caribbean–British Poetry *News For Babylon* and his most recent collection of poems is called *Chain of Days*.

Valerie Bloom was born in Clarendon, Jamaica. She attended Frankfield Primary and High Schools and was trained as a teacher at Mico Teachers' College in Kingston. She taught at Frankfield High School from 1977–79, then came to England and taught Music in Manchester from 1980–82. In 1984 she obtained a First Class Honours degree in English with African and Caribbean Studies from the University of Kent. She appeared on television and radio in England and Jamaica, and performs extensively as well as conducting workshops all over England. Her poems have been included in several anthologies, and her first volume of poetry, *Touch Mi; Tell Mi*, was published by Bogle L'Ouverture in 1983.

Sara Boyes was born in 1945, and has mainly worked in theatre as an actress. She has regularly contributed to poetry magazines, is in a women's writing group and performs poetry as a member of the 'Vera Twins'. Married, with a baby, she lives in London.

Barbara Burford is a medical researcher and has a twelve-year-old daughter. Her poems have appeared in *A Dangerous Knowing; Four Black Women Poets* (Sheba). She has published short stories in *Everyday Matters* (Sheba) and her play *Patterns* was performed in London in 1984. A collection of short stories *The Threshing Floor and other stories* will be published by Sheba this year.

Christopher Cardale (alias Zolan Quobble) was born in 1951. He has worked in a variety of jobs from milkman to undertaker's assistant. He was a member of the 'Worthless Words' and 'Tongue Circus' poetry performance groups. He has performed his poetry widely in venues around the country. He is now a community mosaicist and performance poet and has been a member of the 'Apples & Snakes' collective since 1982. He helped set up and runs the 'Clockhouse Writers'.

Donal Carroll was born in the Republic of Ireland, and has worked at various jobs including labouring, television servicing, teaching. He has written books, articles, reviews, and poetry for various magazines; and has appeared on radio, TV and on the cabaret circuit as a poet/comedian. Coming from a tradition where poetry is not only accepted but expected, he considers much contemporary English poetry is just marinated fragments of elevated whimsy.

Taggart Deike is a poet, playwright, actor and director. His theatre company, 'SubCulture', has travelled to Sheffield, Brighton, Guildford, Cambridge, the Glastonbury Festival, Glasgow and Cardiff, with anti-nuclear plays and shows. He was a member of the 'Angels of Fire' collective for their first two festivals at the Cockpit Theatre. His poems have been published in the festival magazine, and the *Third Eye*. Motto: 'Everything should be done with ceremony.'

Janet Dubé was born in Fulham, London, 1941; schools: Fulham, Hammersmith, Kingston-on-Thames. Teachers' College: Hertford. Further education: evening classes in Wolverhampton, public libraries from Barnet to Caerfyrddin, briefly N. London Poly. Slim volumes: *It'll take a long time* (Onlywomen); *Housewife's Choice, Meditations for our children* (Mustardseeds); *1982, a lament*; (Mustardseeds/XNTrix). Anthologies: *One Foot on the Mountain* (Onlywomen); *Bread and Roses* (Virago). Currently secretary of the Welsh Union of Writers.

Maureen Duffy was born in 1933, and educated at state schools and at King's College, London; she was a teacher for five years before becoming a full-time writer in 1962 with the publication of *That's How It Was*. Since then, she has published twelve novels, four books of poetry, as well as having plays performed and writing non-fiction. Her most recent books are *Gor Saga, Londoners, Men and Beasts: An Animal Rights Handbook*, and her *Collected Poems 1949–1985* which are published by Hamish Hamilton.

Ken Edwards was born in Gibraltar in 1950, and has lived in London since 1968. He has writen poetry, fiction and critical articles in numerous magazines and anthologies; books of poetry include *Lorca: An Elegiac Fragment* (Alembic Editions, 1978); *Tilth* (1980), *Drumming & Poems* (1982) (both Galloping Dog Press). He has been editor of *Reality Studios* since 1978.

Alison Fell was born in 1944 in Scotland. She moved to London in 1970 to work in the Women's Street Theatre Group and later on *Spare Rib*. She now teaches creative writing. She has poetry in several collections, including *Smile Smile Smile Smile* (Sheba) and *Bread and Roses* (Virago). Her novel *Every Move You Make* was published in 1984, by Virago, along with a solo collection of poems, *Kisses For Mayakovsky*. She also contributed an autobiographical piece to *Truth, Dare, Or Promise* – about girls growing up in the '50s (Virago, 1985).

Allen Fisher has been writing poetry since 1967. *Place* project 1971–81 more than five books. Conceptual/performance work 1970s partly with *Fluxus* and including *Blood Bone Brain* multi-media project. Printing, painting, film-making. Over 70 chapbooks and books of poetry and related work, including *Poetry For Schools* (1980); *Unpolished Mirrors* (republished 1985) and *Brixton Fractals* (1985) of which *Banda* is a part.

Berta Freistadt was born in London in 1942 and has written poetry since she was six. Now she writes both poetry and plays in a basement in London fighting for desk space with her cat Lily. In her writing she is concerned to express the deep feminism that proscribes her life. She has read with 'Angels of Fire' four times. She also reads her work with 'Write-Off Poets' and the 'Vera Twins'.

Gandhi Versus The Daleks (place your bets!); London wordsmith/voice/ stage creature, since late seventies/teens co-catalyzin situations sometimes called culture; words can be useful (anti-/pseudo intellectualism costs lives) within dance/politics of awe/desire, reason, dignity/ecstasy etc.? only area of expertise: passionately engaged in some of the problems . . .

Geoffrey Godbert has five collections of poetry published; *The Ides of March* (1975), *The Lover Will Dance Incredibly* (1981), Still Lifes (1983), *The Theatre of Decision* (1985) and most recently *Journey to the Edge of Light: Selected Poems 1965–1985*. He is the co-publisher of The Greville Press and a new radical poetry imprint, The Diamond Press. He has been editor of two poetry magazines *Only Poetry* and *The Third Eye*, and was on the organising collective of the second 'Angels of Fire' festival.

Paul A. Green. Poetry publications include *Basement Mix* (Galloping Dog) and *The Slow Ceremony* (Spectacular Diseases) plus numerous appearances in mags – and on stage, often with musician Vincent Crane. Other work includes fiction, and stage/radio drama e.g. *The Dream Laboratory* (CBC), *Ritual of the Stifling Air* (BBC) and *Power Play* (Capital/ILR), as well as criticism/polemic for *City Limits*, *Third Eye*, *Reality Studios*, among others.

Bill Griffiths is the man behind Pirate Press. He has worked closely with many other experimental writers and with the Association of Little Presses. Other work includes Ripe Tapes – a sound poetry series, and Pyrofiche – a microfiche project. Recent publications include *The Death of Guthlac* (from Spectacular Diseases) – a translation of the old English poem 'Guthlac B'.

Graham Hartill has run creative writing workshops in Merthyr Tydfil and in Cardiff. He edits and produces the cassette magazine *Flying in the Face*, he has had several collections of poetry published, most recently *Songs: From the Purple Mountain* (Spectacular Diseases, 1984). From 1984–85 he spent a year teaching English literature to graduate students at Nankai University Tienjin, China.

Libby Houston was born in 1941. Her work has been published in three collections, *A Stained Glass Raree Show*, *Plain Clothes* and *At the Mercy*, and she is a regular contributor of programmes of poetry for children to the BBC Schools series, *Pictures in Your Mind*. Tutor for the Arvon Foundation for many years, she founded the workshop *Practising Poets* in Bristol where she currently lives with her two children.

Nicki Jackowska has published four collections of poetry and two novels, her most recent poetry collection is *Gates to the City* (Taxus Press, 1985). Her poetry and prose have appeared in many publications over the last fifteen years including *Ambit*, *Argo* and *Stand*, she has read her work widely at festivals, concerts and cabarets as well as on BBC radio.

Alan Jackson: BORN, MASSACRED, LOVED, DIED, STILL HERE. He has published many books and pamphlets since the late '6os, among them *The Grim Wayfarer* (Fulcrum Press), *Penguin Modern Poets (12)*, and *The Guardians Have Arrived* (Ten To Six Press, 1978). Recent pamphlets include *Star Child* and *To Stand Against The Wind*. Following a period of deliberate absence from the Lit. Scene he is back on the edges of it, on his own terms; and having lived for a time out in the wilds in Perthshire, is at present back at home in Edinburgh. His Selected Poems, *Heart Of The Sun*, is forthcoming from Open Township.

Mahmood Jamal was born in 1948 in India and came to Britain in 1967. Co-ordinated readings at the Troubadour Coffee House, 1972–75 and participated in 'Black Voices', a forum for Third World writers. First published with three other poets in *Coins For Charon* (Courtfield Press, 1976). A solo collection, *Silence Inside A Gun's Mouth*, was published by the Kala Press in 1984 to celebrate London Against Racism Year. At present he is performing his poetry, and translating modern Urdu poetry into English for publication by Penguin in 1986.

Keith Jefferson – Actor, Playwright, Poet, Teacher, Musician, was born in 1951 in Kansas City. He has been featured in many US and UK publications. His *The Hyena Reader* (Black River Writers) came out in 1975. He was amongst the original 'Angels of Fire' posse, is included in the first two anthologies, and can be heard on the 'Knife In The Light' tape. He is married with a little boy named Zen.

Desmond Johnson was born in Kingston, Jamaica, in 1962 and came to London in 1980 where he lives and works. His first full-length collection of poems, *Deadly Ending Season* (Akira Press, 1984), has been published to much critical acclaim. He works as a founder-director of Akira Press, publishers.

Jackie Kay has written *Since Agnes Left*, a short story, which is to be published by Pandora this year in a collection of 'celebratory' women's short stories. Some of her new poems are to be published in *Charting The Journey*, a Black women's anthology to be published by Sheba at the beginning of 1986. At the moment she is working on a play provisionally entitled *The Meeting Place* to be performed by the Theatre of Black Women. She is also still working on her first novel and on a new collection of poems.

Judith Kazantzis was born in 1940. Neurotic-intuitive poet/thinker, concerned with feminism, egalitarian simple non-stop philosophy, and stopping

War (see birthdate); her books of poetry include *Minefield* (1977), *Wicked Queen* (Sidgwick & Jackson, 1980), *Touchpapers* (with Michèle Roberts & Michelene Wandor, Allison & Busby, 1982) and *Let's Pretend* (Virago, 1984). She also works as a teacher for ILEA students.

Deborah Levy was born in 1959 and is a playwright, poet, and performer. Her plays include *Ophelia And The Great Idea, Clam,* and *Pax* (which travelled recently to the USA). She has had poems published in a wide variety of magazines, and in a joint collection *A Singing In The Throat* (with Mina Loy).

Dinah Livingstone has lived in Camden Town since 1966; she has three children. She often performs her poems in London and elsewhere. She won Arts Council Writer's Awards in 1969, 1975 and 1978. Her poems have been published in magazines and anthologies including *Arts Council 1, PEN 77, Eve before the Holocaust, Apples and Snakes, Voices from Arts for Labour;* collected in pamphlets including *Ultrasound* (1974); *Prepositions* and *Conjunctions* (1977); *Love in Time* (1982); *Glad Rags* (1983); *Something Understood* (1985) (Katabasis).

Tony Lopez was born in Stockwell, South London in 1950. He published five novels with the New English Library in the '70s before going as a mature student to Essex University. His most recent publications are *A Handbook Of British Birds* (Pig Press, 1981), *Abstract & Delicious* (Secret Books, 1982) and his perform-ance documentary *New Zone West* (Actual Size, 1983) which illustrates his concern as a performance artist with the relation of poetry to other media.

Lindsay MacRae was born in Yorkshire in 1961. She has studied drama, film and television. She has played the saxophone in several bands, has been a newsreader for Vatican Radio, and is a regular performer of her work on the London cabaret circuit. She is presently working on a film script. Her publications include two anthologies, *No Holds Barred* (Women's Press) and *Purple and Green* (Rivelin Grapheme). She is a member of the Angels of Fire collective.

Sue May was born in London in 1955. She writes poetry, short stories and reviews, and since 1978 has been a member of the Hackney Writers' Workshop. She also reads with the 'Vera Twins' and 'Contradictions'. Some of her work has been published in *Bird turning the sky, Where there's smoke, Hackney Writers Workshop 3* and *Everyday Matters.* Also in the magazines *City Limits, Spare Rib* and *Jazz Journal.* She lives in London, not too far from The Angel, Islington.

Mary Michaels was born in 1946 and lives and works in London. Her work has appeared in a number of magazines and anthologies and she has published two small collections: *In Bédar* (1979) and *Twelve Poems* (1983). She was a member of the feminist exhibition group 'Sister Seven' and has reviewed poetry for *City Limits* magazine.

Lotte Moos was born in 1909. Her first book of poems was published in 1981. Before that, a number of her poems appeared in anthologies of the Hackney Writers' Workshop, in *Women Their World*, and she won a prize at the Lancaster Literature Festival (1980). She contributed poems to the Cut and Thrust Cabaret (Drill Hall, 1983). A second book of her poems is now in the hands of the publishers.

Cheryl Moskowitz was born in Chicago, Illinois in 1959. She studied Developmental Psychology and has worked as an actress and a teacher in education. As well as writing poetry, she also writes plays and short stories. She has been a member of the 'Angels of Fire' collective since the end of 1984.

Wendy Mulford was born in World War Two, and was brought up in Wales. She has been in Cambridge from the '60s onwards, and has taught since 1968. She ran Street Editions from 1972–80; and her own books include *Bravo To Girls & Heroes* (1977), *The Light Sleepers* (1980), *Reactions To Sunsets* (1980), *Some Poems* (with Denise Riley, 1982), and *River Whose Eyes* (1982). Work forthcoming includes *The ABC Of Writing & Other Poems* (Torque Press), *The East Anglia Sequence* (Spectacular Diseases) and *Poems 1978–1984* (Loxwood Stoneleigh).

H. O. Nazareth was born in India, and grew up there, before coming to Britain in 1965. He has worked as writer and producer on several video/films, including the play *The Garland* (1981, for BBC), *Music Fusion* (1982, for C4), and *Talking History: CLR James & EP Thomson* (first shown at ICA, 1983). He has also worked as a journalist, specialising in Third World culture and history, for *The Guardian*, *New Statesman*, *The Times Of India*, and *City Limits*, amongst others. *Lobo*, a collection of his poems, was published in 1984. He is at present working on *London Settlers* (interviews) for Pluto Press.

Grace Nichols won the Commonwealth Poetry Prize for her *I is A Long Memoried Woman*. Her most recent collection is *The Fat Black Woman's Poems* (Virago) and her first novel for adults, *Whole of A Morning Sky*, is also to be published by Virago.

Pascale Petit was born in Paris in 1953 and is currently studying at the Royal College of Art for an MA in sculpture. She has already exhibited in the major touring show 'Pandora's Box'. Her poetry and sculpture have been filmed for television and the ICA. Poems and short stories have appeared in *Iron, Writing Women, Litmus, Strange Mathematics, Graffiti, Ad Astra,* and an anthology published by Edward Arnold.

Stef Pixner was born in London in 1945. Educated at Leeds and the LSE, she worked in a wide range of occupations from gardener to polytechnic lecturer. Her latest collection of poetry is *Sawdust and White Spirit* (Virago).

Michèle Roberts was born in 1949 of a French mother and an English father. Her most recent novel is *The Wild Girl* (Methuen, 1984) and her *The Mirror of The Mother* (Methuen, 1986) was published early this year. She is currently completing her fourth novel and a work of non-fiction.

Valerie Sinason was born in 1946, is a child psychotherapist, English lecturer and poet. Her work has appeared widely in such places as Thames TV, Radio 3 Poetry Now, *Spare Rib, Literary Review, Outposts, Iron, Ambit, Bread and Roses* (Virago), *Tribune, P.E.N.* etc. She has read her work in many settings and edits *Gallery* magazine. She is married and has two children.

Janet Sutherland was born in 1957 in Salisbury. She went to university in Cardiff and Essex and then worked for three years for a clothing firm in Islington. She currently works for Hackney Council, job-sharing to allow more time for writing. Her poetry has appeared in many magazines including *Strange Mathematics, Telegram, Angel Exhaust* and *Reality Studios*. She frequently reviews poetry for *City Limits* magazine and has a collection of poems published, *Crossing Over* (NoSuch Press, 1983).

Penelope Toff is a psychology graduate, studying medicine and trying with others to develop a holistic approach to health-care. She was a founder member of the 'Angels of Fire' collective, co-editor of the *A of F* magazines and worked on the production team of *Strange Mathematics*. Her writing and artwork have appeared in small press publications and in *Purple and Green: Poems by 33 Women Poets* (Rivelin Grapheme, 1985).

Chris Torrance was born in 1941 in Edinburgh. He has been a fulltime poet in Wales since 1970, and a lecturer in Creative Writing for the Extra-Mural Dept. of University College, Cardiff. His main writings have been in *The Magic Door* books I–V. He is also co-founder of a poetry & music band POETHEAT.

Michelene Wandor was born in 1940. From 1971–82 she was Poetry Editor and theatre critic for *Time Out* magazine. Her publications include *Upbeat* (1982) and *Gardens of Eden* (1984), both poetry collections; *Understudies*: on theatre and sexual politics (Routledge); *Five Plays* (Journeyman Press). She has written many plays, features and dramatisations for radio and theatre. *Guests in the Body*, a collection of stories, is published by Virago.

Frederick Williams was born in St Thomas, Jamaica, in 1947. He joined his parents in England when he was sixteen, and now works for British Railways. His publications include *Moving Up* (1978) and *Me Memba Wen* (1981). His most recent collection, *Leggo de Pen*, was published by Akira Press in 1985.

Mark Williams was born in 1952. He currently lives in Balham and teaches at Her Majesty's Prisons of Wandsworth and Pentonville, and the City Lit. He has had two collections of poetry published, *The Book of Noman* (NoSuch Press, 1983) and *Reading The Distance* (KQBX, 1984).

ACKNOWLEDGEMENTS

For permission to reprint copyright material the publishers gratefully acknowledge the following:

Bananas for 'Kite' by Sara Boyes; Hamish Hamilton Ltd for 'Chattel' by Maureen Duffy from her *Collected Poems 1949–84;* Balsam Flex, Cardiff, for 'Lexical Dub, for Sarah Tisdall' by Ken Edwards, which was released on a stereo cassette in 1984; Spanner/Open Field no. 1, 1983, for an extract from 'Banda' (lines 1–137) by Allen Fisher, including fragments from Olivier Messiaen's work on birds; Only Poetry Publications for 'The world has yet to be named' by Geoffrey Godbert which first appeared in *The Lover Will Dance Incredibly,* 1981; *DNA* cassette magazine, distributed by Laurence Russell, for 'Directions' by Paul A. Green; *Slow Dancer* for 'Childe Roland' by Libby Houston; Ten to Six Press for 'This is it' by Alan Jackson, which appeared in *The Guardians have Arrived* 1978; Coconut Mania for 'Red Rosa' by Deborah Levy which first appeared in *Change Of State* (1984), and *Ambit* for 'Philosophers'; *Strange Mathematics* for 'Nerve' and *Angels of Fire* for 'Peace' by Dinah Livingstone. These also appeared in her book, *Something Understood;* Secret Books for 'Poem about Swallows' by Tony Lopez which first appeared in *Abstract and Delicious,* 1982; *Argo* for 'The Ice Land' and *Writing Women* for 'Dream and Five Interpretations' by Mary Michaels; Hackney Writers' Workshop for 'Joy' by Lotte Moos which appeared in their anthology, and which also featured in the author's book *Time to be Bold;* Torque Press for 'How do you live?' by Wendy Mulford which first appeared in *The ABC of Writing and Poems* in 1985; *Lobo* (London and Bombay 1984) for 'The Promised Land' by H. O. Nazareth; Virago Press for 'Whose Fault' and 'Near Death' by Stef Pixner which first appeared in *Sawdust and White Spirit; Cabaret 246* for 'I see' by Chris Torrance; *Strange Mathematics* and KQBX Press for 'Descriptive poem' by Mark Williams.

ILLUSTRATION ACKNOWLEDGEMENTS

Sculpture and photograph by Pascale Petit, page 113; aquatint, 'Jug and Bottle XIII' by Allen Fisher, page 124; photograph of swan's feather by Carole Bruce, page 140.

INDEX OF POETS AND WORKS